What defendants neec

Sentencing

In *Prepare,* readers learn:

- » How to Understand Criminal Proceedings
- » How to work effectively with a defense attorney
- » Factors to consider pleading to an offense
- » How a conviction influences earning power
- » To influence a presentence investigation report
- » How mitigation packages influence sentencing
- » How to prepare for sentencing
- » How to understand First Step Act
- » How to make progress in prison
- » About collateral consequences of convictions

Regardless of whether a person has been charged with a DWI, a misdemeanor, or a felony conviction, in this era of mass incarceration, sanctions can be severe. When readers learn how to prepare early, they may start a self-advocacy campaign that can lead to the least burdensome sanction possible.

For more details, visit

www.ResilientCourses.com

Prepare:

What defendants need to know about Lawyers / Mitigation / Sentencing / Prison / The First Step Act

Justin Paperny
With Michael Santos

ISBN: 9781082190452

For more information, visit www.ResilientCourses.com

Or contact:

Justin Paperny
Info@ResilientCourses.com

I dedicate this book to my loving wife
Sandra Paperny,
and to our two children, Alyssa and Jason.

Justin Paperny

I dedicate this book to my loving wife,
Carole Santos,
and to the many people that believed in us.

Michael Santos

Other Books by Resilient Courses Authors

Inside: Life Behind Bars in America
(St. Martin's Press)

About Prison
(Wadsworth/Thompson Press)

Profiles From Prison
(Greenwood/Praeger Publishing)

Prison! My 8,344th Day
(Resilient Courses)

Success! The Straight-A Guide
(Resilient Courses)

Triumph!
The Straight-A Guide: Conquering Imprisonment
(Resilient Courses)

Earning Freedom
(Resilient Courses)

Lessons from Prison
(Resilient Courses)

Ethics in Motion
(Resilient Courses)

Living Deliberately
(Resilient Courses)

Resilient
(Resilient Courses)

Visit: www.ResilientCourses.com for more information

Table of Contents

Chapter 1

What if I Become the Target of a Criminal Investigation?

If you've become the target of a criminal investigation, you need to know a lot: life is about to change in dramatic ways.

Many people that face law-enforcement challenges make decisions that exacerbate their problems. They don't mean to make troubles worse. Yet if they don't understand what's coming, what options they have, or where to turn for information that will help them make better decisions, they're vulnerable.

Targets of criminal investigations can unwittingly talk themselves into a criminal indictment. They may eliminate opportunities for a diversion from prosecution. Or they may expose themselves to tougher sanctions.

Competent legal counsel is essential. But if an individual doesn't have any experience with the criminal law, a primer on the system may be of help, too. With more knowledge, a layman will feel more competent when working with a criminal lawyer. Without knowledge, a person will always feel as if he's operating from a position of darkness, never knowing what's around the next turn.

By learning about the criminal justice system, a person can arm himself to work more effectively with lawyers. He may understand how to resolve complex dilemmas better.

Although he may not like the limited choices available, he may feel more confident that he is going to make the best possible choice. When a person understands context, opportunity costs, and ramifications that follow each decision, that person empowers himself.

We can paraphrase an old Chinese proverb:

» If you want to know the road ahead, ask someone that has come back.

When under the spotlight of a criminal investigation, it makes a great deal of sense to invest time and energy to learn. By learning, a person can make more informed decisions. Operating without knowledge makes us feel as if we're hanging from a string, as if we're marionette puppets. To stop that helpless feeling and restore confidence, we need to learn, then we need to make deliberate decisions that will influence best-possible outcomes.

Acquiring knowledge and becoming more literate about the system is a first step. As the cliché holds, the greatest fear is the fear of the unknown.

This book will be a great place to start.

Defendants learn quickly that problems with the criminal justice system can lead to enormous costs. It isn't only money that's at stake. Liberty is at stake. Future earning power is at stake. Collateral consequences—like access to banking, housing, career opportunities—can linger for a lifetime. Don't take our word for it. Easily verifiable statistics show the fallout for those who have been targeted by the criminal justice system.

It's crucial to prepare, and it makes a great deal of

sense to learn.

The learning process begins with the reality that many people get sucked into the criminal justice system. Although going through the system is difficult, there are best-practice ways to prepare.

According to a 2019 report by the Prison Policy Initiative, the American criminal justice system holds almost 2.3 million people. They are confined to:

- » 1,719 state prisons,
- » 109 federal prisons,
- » 1,772 juvenile correctional facilities,
- » 3,163 local jails, and

Eighty Indian Country jails as well as in military prisons, immigration detention facilities, civil commitment centers, state psychiatric hospitals, and prisons in the U.S. territories.

Not everyone that goes into the system gets the best outcome. Those that learn more can prepare more. By learning more about the system, they may be able to put themselves into a different algorithm, framing possibilities for a better outcome.

By using good critical thinking skills, targets or defendants may influence decision makers to view them through a different lens, as if they're fellow human beings rather than cogs that must grind through a criminal justice machine.

All people facing challenges with the criminal justice system share common traits. Their family members, friends, and colleagues care about them.

Defendants would like to live in a world where investigators, prosecutors, probation officers, and judges see them as normal citizens. They may have been charged with a crime, but defendants, like all people, have many attributes that are reflective of their character. A crime may be an aberration, a one-time act that is contextual and doesn't resemble how they would act in most circumstances.

Yet once the criminal justice system targets people for prosecution, stakeholders in the system turn their attention to the alleged criminal wrongdoing. A criminal charge can stop stakeholders from looking at an individual as a human being. In an instant, the person becomes a defendant. The goal, or objective is not always justice. It's a conviction followed by a punitive sanction.

Obviously, targets of criminal investigations would like to find some type of diversionary program to avoid prosecution. If they're prosecuted, they want the best possible outcome. For most people, the best outcome means the least restrictive or least punitive sanction—preferably a sentence that does not include incarceration.

But how does a person go about getting the best outcome? Unfortunately, statistics show that few people that encounter the criminal justice system know how to position themselves for the best possible result.

Who Are We?

My name is Justin Paperny. I'm the director of White Collar Advice and Prison Professors, two websites that I created with my partners, Shon Hopwood and Michael Santos. Both of my partners have extensive experience in the criminal justice system.

Shon is a law professor at the Georgetown Law School, in Washington D.C. But he didn't always have such a distinguished role. As a young man he made some bad decisions, as he wrote in his book *Law Man*. When Shon was 20, he participated in a series of five armed-bank robberies.

It's kind of weird to think of Shon as being a convicted bank robber. A judge sentenced him to serve 12 years in federal prison for his crimes. While in prison, he began working to reconcile, trying to make things right by living as a good and contributing citizen.

In his book *Law Man: Memoir of a Jailhouse Lawyer*, available in paperback from our website, Shon tells his full story. Readers can learn how we can always begin sowing seeds for a better outcome when we start making better decisions. Few people get to leave prison with the type of outcomes that characterize Shon's journey:

» Graduated from college

» Scholarship to law school

» Clerked for a federal appeals court

» Became a licensed attorney

» Earned an advanced law degree from Georgetown

» Became a professor at one of the top law schools in the world, and

» Worked with Congress and the White House on policy reforms.

Shon has worked and others have recognized his accomplishments. They see and consider him for the good decisions he made after his conviction, rather than for the crime that led him to prison.

For that reason, Shon has written that he feels compelled to work toward reforms. And we would argue that he has made a massive contribution to systemic change, opening possibilities for others to get better outcomes.

Those who've been targeted by the criminal justice should know options and opportunities that are open to them, at the soonest possible time. Then they can make more informed decisions on how to proceed.

As Yogi Berra said:

» If you don't know where you're going, you'll end up someplace else.

Like Shon, my other partner has extensive experience in the criminal justice system. Michael made bad decisions when he was in his early 20s. He sold cocaine. As a result the bad decisions he made, a judge sentenced Michael to serve a lengthy prison term.

He started serving his sentence on August 11, 1987 and he didn't complete his prison term until August 12, 2013. He was a prisoner for 26 years, and he served time in prisons of every security level.

Despite multiple decades in prison, Michael led a productive life. He earned a bachelor's degree from Mercer University and a master's degree from Hofstra University. He published several books to help others learn more about the criminal justice system, as well to teach strategies others can use to emerge successfully.

Since concluding his prison term, Michael has launched and built several businesses, and he's always been a resource to me.

I'm a graduate of USC, and a former securities broker. I made bad decisions in my career, which led to my conviction for violating securities laws. While incarcerated, I met Michael Santos and we began working together. I authored two books, including *Lessons from Prison* and *Ethics in Motion*. Upon my release from prison, I began building a career around all that I learned, and authored a third book, *Living Deliberately*.

Through our consulting firms, I've interacted with federal judges, prosecutors, defense attorneys, and more than 1,000 people that have experienced the criminal justice system. I'm a public speaker, a reputation management consultant, and an expert on rebuilding after struggle.

» White Collar Advice

» Prison Professors

» Resilient Courses

Through our various websites and social media platforms, we offer products, courses, and services. When people anticipate that authorities may target them for prosecution, members of our team can help.

Although we don't offer legal advice, we're well connected with lawyers and law firms that can help. Those looking for guidance on post-conviction matters, including sentences and appeals, may want to connect with our partner Shon at The Hopwood Law

Firm.

Each of us has extensive experience in going through the system and getting best outcomes. Together, we help people that want to help themselves. Anyone who is in the unfortunate position of being targeted by criminal investigators would do well to learn more.

Overview:

Relatively few Americans have more than a basic understanding of our nation's criminal justice system. On the surface, people know that law enforcement officers arrest people, prosecutors bring charges, and some defendants who are convicted go to jail or prison. Yet the system is much more complicated than that, with many moving parts.

Targets should begin from the premise that the system has one function: to protect society. It has a series of procedures designed to enforce the laws of this country. The more we understand about the system, the better we can prepare to navigate the challenges.

All branches of law enforcement work together to prosecute crimes. Just as some offenders will make every effort to evade detection and apprehension by law-enforcement, the different members of law enforcement will make every effort to solve a crime and win a conviction.

As citizens, we're all charged with the responsibility of abiding by our nation's laws. Legislators pass the bills and heads of state sign the bills into law. It's the criminal justice system that is responsible for enforcing the laws.

Few people understand that our country has 53

separate criminal justice systems, including one for each state, one for the District of Columbia, one for the military, and one for the federal government. Within the different systems, there are hundreds of jurisdictions, each with a series of trial courts that make findings of fact. Higher courts may review whether trial courts followed accepted procedures.

This elaborately complex system has evolved over hundreds of years. For a person that enters the system, it can feel like he's been dropped into a byzantine labyrinth, with so many turns and dimensions that make it easy to lose direction.

To put this into perspective, think of the system as a zero-sum game.

We use the metaphor of a game for clarity, not to trivialize the conflict between accused and accuser. Defendants are the opponents of investigators and prosecutors. Both sides want to win.

The defendants want to be diverted from prosecutions, acquitted, or receive the least restrictive sanction. Law enforcement officers want to convict. Prosecutors want to ensure that the defendants receive what they deem as an appropriate sanction.

In this "*game*" of criminal justice, the judge acts as a referee. Judges strive to ensure that both sides of the game adhere to the rules, or due process. They must follow established procedures within the system.

In some instances, juries will determine the outcome of this game. But in most cases, defendants will plead guilty before a judge. Then, the long game begins, with post-conviction proceedings.

They include a pre-sentence investigation and a

sentencing hearing. Classification processes follow. For some, the next step includes appeals, imprisonment, supervised release, and all of the collateral consequences that stay with the "felon" class.

The sooner a target, or a defendant starts preparing, the more influence that person can have on a better outcome.

As Mick Jagger sang, we don't always get what we want. But if we try sometimes, we just might find, we get what we need. To get what we need, we must work with a criminal defense attorney. And the more we know about what is to come, the better we prepare ourselves to help our lawyers get us the best outcome.

For example, if we know what follows in prison, we may be in a better position to understand the impact of a plea agreement or a prison term. In all cases, knowledge can help us make more informed decisions and restore confidence.

In the next chapter, we'll cover some thoughts to consider when working with a criminal defense attorney.

Chapter 2

What Should I Consider Before I Hire a Criminal Defense Lawyer?

In the first chapter, we emphasized the complexities of the legal system. With myriad codes, decisions, procedures, guidelines, and jurisdictions, hiring a lawyer makes a lot of sense if a person faces any type of legal challenge. When nonexperts respond to the legal system without counsel, they can lose their rights or expose themselves to further problems. Even experienced attorneys hire lawyers when they anticipate that they may face problems from the legal system.

Since the legal system is so broad, attorneys tend to specialize in one or more practice areas. An attorney that specializes in taxation, for example, would likely know a great deal about the tax code and how to create structures that minimize liability.

Yet a tax lawyer may not know much about federal criminal procedure. Likewise, a lawyer that works exclusively on sentencing matters in federal criminal court may not be the best attorney to hire if that person wants to negotiate a severance agreement with an employer.

With the law, as with any profession, it's crucial to hire experts.

Hiring Specialists:

If someone learns that a representative of law enforcement is asking questions, that is a good sign that an investigation is underway. And it's a good sign that the person needs a lawyer. The investigation may be civil, with questions from representatives of the SEC, the FTC, or state regulators. Since civil investigations frequently lead to criminal indictments, it's crucial to get appropriate guidance at the soonest possible time.

When the questions come from the FBI or DEA, the problem is more immediate. That's an obvious sign that a criminal investigation has begun. In either case, whether questions are coming from civil or criminal investigators, the time is ripe to begin researching lawyers.

As the cliché holds, in the land of the blind, the one-eyed man is king. It may be normal to call a friend or acquaintance to ask for free legal advice if a person learns that government regulators are asking questions. That friend may be a business lawyer, divorce lawyer, or labor lawyer.

Obviously, any licensed attorney knows more about the law than a layman. Yet if a person lacks subject-matter expertise—even if the person practices law in another area—consider asking for a recommendation for an expert rather than asking for legal advice about a case that could potentially lead to criminal charges.

If a person has been charged with a crime, that criminal charge removes ambiguity. With any criminal charge, a person's liberty, livelihood, and reputation will be at stake. Defendants know:

» The jurisdiction,

» The type of charge, and to some extent,

» The potential exposure.

A person that faces a state charge for vehicular manslaughter would do well to hire a lawyer that specializes in criminal law, in the specific jurisdiction. On the other hand, a defendant that has been indicted for fraud in federal court requires a lawyer that specializes in white-collar criminal defense, with expertise in federal criminal proceedings and federal sentencing.

Given available resources, take affirmative steps to choose the right lawyer, in the right jurisdiction, with the right expertise.

Bars and Jurisdictions:

Each state has a professional association of lawyers that is known as the state bar. The state bar is responsible for issuing licenses to qualified members and overseeing how they practice law in a specific jurisdiction. To become a licensed attorney in any given state, our understanding is that a person must:

» Graduate from a law school accredited by the American Bar Association,

» Pass the state bar exam, and

» Have the appropriate moral character—as determined by the bar association—to represent others in a court of law.

Besides requiring a lawyer to have a license from the state bar, courts may also require a lawyer to go through additional screening or training in order to practice in a specific jurisdiction.

What is a jurisdiction?

In the first chapter, we noted that the United States has many criminal justice systems. Each state has its own criminal code, and each state is its own jurisdiction. Different levels of trial courts resolve disputes, or find facts, in each state system. The states will have an intermediate appellate court that reviews trial court decisions. And each state will have a high court that reviews appellate court decisions.

The federal government trumps state courts, with the U.S. Supreme Court being the highest court in the land. Beneath the Supreme Court, our country has 13 separate circuit courts. The circuit courts are regional appellate courts, overseeing a specific portion of the 94 district courts spread across the entire country. In the 94 separate federal district-court jurisdictions, more than 800 federal judges preside over findings of fact.

Several thousand judges (some appointed, some elected) preside over several hundred jurisdictions in state and federal courts across the country. A lawyer that specializes in one jurisdiction may or may not have expertise in another jurisdiction.

For example, a lawyer that specializes in California state court may not be as familiar with federal sentencing law, which requires very specific knowledge.

When hiring a lawyer, individuals should consider what level of expertise the prospective lawyer has in a specific jurisdiction, and in the domain that applies to the specific type of case.

Public Defenders:

In 1963, the U.S. Supreme Court issued a landmark ruling known as *Gideon v. Wainwright*. With the *Gideon* case, the Court found that all people who have been charged with serious offenses have a Constitutional right to a lawyer. If a defendant cannot afford a lawyer, the Court will appoint a licensed attorney at no charge to the defendant.

Before appointing counsel to represent a defendant, the Court may require the defendant to submit a financial statement. After reviewing the defendant's ability to pay, the court will make a ruling on whether the defendant qualifies for appointed counsel.

Qualifying for appointed counsel does not necessarily mean that the defendant is utterly impoverished. It simply means that after reviewing the defendant's finances, the Court agrees that the defendant does not have sufficient financial capacity to hire an attorney. The court will then turn to the public defender's office, or the bar association to hire a lawyer that will represent the defendant.

Regardless of whether the court pays for the lawyer, or the defendant pays for the lawyer, a licensed attorney has a fiduciary duty to represent the defendant. In other words, the lawyer has a legal and ethical responsibility to represent the defendant to the best of his or her ability.

Many lawyers aspire to build careers as public defenders, suggesting that they place a high value on social justice and assisting people in need.

Despite having to manage extensive caseloads, public defenders are often extremely effective advocates for their clients. They have access to an abundance of training and resources. Further, hey frequently limit their representation to specific types of cases in specific jurisdictions.

Although a defendant has a Constitutional right to counsel, the defendant does not have a right to his specific choice of counsel. Many times, defendants find fault with the lawyer because the lawyer isn't available to answer every question, or to provide the support a person craves during a difficult time.

When a court appoints an attorney to represent a defendant, the defendant should work to understand the role of the attorney, and to assist the attorney by striving to provide a narrative of what transpired.

Defendants are wise to remember that an attorney will not have all of the facts. Instead, the attorney will have to come up to speed by reading information in the charging instrument, and learning more from evidence collected through the process. The defendant can help the attorney get more context, but it will take time for the defense attorney to understand the complexities of the full story.

The attorney will assess evidence and the prosecution's ability to prove a case, reviewing charges and the evidence. Meanwhile, the defendant has a responsibility to speak honestly, providing background, context, and any evidence that may exonerate or mitigate the charges. The more effectively a defendant can help an attorney understand what happened, the more a defendant empowers the attorney to build a defense.

On the other hand, defense attorneys may not be in the best position to help defendants grasp the implications of a conviction. For example, the defense attorney may not be able to speak with certainty about what happens after a sentencing hearing.

If the defendant wants to know all the implications of a 60-month sentence, there will be factors that are outside a defense attorney's scope of practice. A defense attorney may not be the best source of information to respond to such questions as:

- » Where will I serve my sentence?
- » What will the atmosphere be like in the prison where I serve time?
- » What types of programs will be available in prison?
- » What can I do before I go in to qualify for the best programs?
- » How will the First Step Act influence my life in prison?
- » What can I do to live productively in prison?
- » How can I manage my business while I'm in prison?
- » How will my day be structured while I serve time?
- » What will happen with my financial affairs while I'm in prison?
- » How will I rebuild my life after I'm released?
- » What can I do to position myself for the highest level of liberty once I get out?

Finding answers to those types of questions may help a defendant make a more informed decision when considering how to respond to a criminal charge.

Retaining Counsel:

When retaining counsel, it's important to think about a budget. Ordinarily, attorneys bill by the hour. The hourly rate will depend upon a lawyer's experience, reputation, jurisdiction, and area of expertise. In some jurisdictions, lawyers may work for less than $200 per hour.

In other jurisdictions, lawyers with specific expertise may charge more than $2,000 per hour, in accordance with market rates. In jurisdictions like New York City, Washington DC, or San Francisco, defendants should expect to pay higher rates than in more rural jurisdictions. After all, office space in those cities is much more expensive than in cities like Tuscaloosa, Gary, and Jackson.

Whether a lawyer charges $200 per hour or $2,000 per hour, defendants should anticipate that hiring a lawyer will be a significant investment. The investment does not guarantee a victory in Court, or the outcome that a defendant wants. But it should guarantee the best possible representation, given the resources available to deal with facts and evidence of the case.

When hiring counsel, consider the duties and responsibilities of a lawyer. In order to provide "the best possible representation," lawyers must review every piece of evidence that prosecutors will consider.

If there are multiple defendants in a case, the lawyers may have to review evidence against all of the defendants. Lawyers enhance their value by reviewing case law, statutes, rules of procedure, and judicial decisions that may or may not have anything to do with the case at hand. Lawyers may need to hire investigators, expert witnesses, or they may need to depose potential witnesses.

Defendants that hire counsel should expect lawyers to bill in accordance with their hourly rate for every minute they devote to the case. Those high hourly rates allow the lawyer to continue learning, *or practicing*, by staying current with relevant decisions—even though they're not billing for that time. If more than one lawyer is working on a case, the defendant should expect to pay hourly rates for multiple lawyers.

Before hiring counsel, defendants should consider their financial resources and be realistic about the length of time a lawyer will need to prepare. A defendant may have specific facts and know the origins of the case. Yet lawyers approach a case with a blank slate. They may offer a free consultation, but to truly mount a defense, they need to invest considerable amounts of time.

Defendants should expect to pay for that time, which can lead to legal fees that are much higher than the defendant expected.

Lawyers will have to sift through evidence. They may have to listen to telephone recordings that, cumulatively, last for dozens of hours. If the government confiscated computer files, there may be thousands of emails or text messages to read. Lawyers may need to interview witnesses, or review transcripts of what witnesses said in other proceedings.

To prepare a case effectively, lawyers can easily devote hundreds of hours. If multiple lawyers are assigned to a case, the bill may show thousands of hours, depending on complexity. Without sufficient preparation, a lawyer may not be able to give an accurate assessment of the best possible outcome. They may not even be able to advise whether it makes sense to proceed through trial or pursue a plea agreement.

Conflicts and Retainer Agreements:

In some cases, judges will not allow a lawyer to withdraw from a case after a lawyer signs on to represent a criminal defendant. For that reason, lawyers typically take a risk-averse approach when choosing which defendants to represent. They will not want to represent new clients that could potentially conflict with their representation of other clients.

Lawyers may ask defendants to sign "retainer agreements" before they accept a defendant as a client. The retainer agreement should detail hourly rates for each person or position that may work on the case. Partners may work at one hourly rate, associate lawyers may work at other hourly rates, paralegals may work at other hourly rates, and investigators may work at other hourly rates.

The retainer agreement may require the defendant to deposit a specific amount of money into the lawyer's trust account. The defendant consummates the agreement by signing a contract and depositing funds into the lawyer's trust account.

The lawyer should keep detailed records, recording how much time each person on the lawyer's team devotes to the case. At the end of the billing cycle, whether weekly, bi-weekly, or monthly, the law firm should create a statement showing billable hours. The lawyer will transfer funds (from the retainer) out of his trust account into his business-operating account to get paid for those billable hours. Some lawyers require the defendant to replenish the trust account with more funds at the start of each month, as specified in the retainer agreement.

The retainer agreement may also include language that allows the lawyer "to fire" the defendant. That means the lawyer may cite reasons why the lawyer does not want to work with the client further.

Our team has worked with some lawyers that absolutely refuse to work with a client that hires outside consultants. Some defense attorneys do not want the client getting information from anywhere other than from the attorney. Yet, those same defense attorneys may not be available to respond to the defendant's questions about what to expect.

Plea Agreements:

All defendants have a constitutional right to plead not guilty and pursue the case in court. Scorched-earth defense strategies, however, can come at a high cost. With legal fees for trial that can easily rise to hundreds of thousands of dollars, and the threat of more onerous sanctions for those found guilty after trial, the vast majority of defendants settle criminal charges with plea agreements.

Prosecutors and defense attorneys may or may not be amenable to settling a case early. Sometimes, lawyers find it advantageous to push prosecutors to the limit in strategic acts of brinksmanship. If prosecutors believe that the defense team may be able to prevail, they may be more receptive to a favorable plea agreement. On the flip side, prosecutors may want to settle cases early in order to preserve prosecutorial resources.

In the federal system, prosecutors resolve the vast majority of cases with plea agreements. In exchange for the defendant's admission of guilt, prosecutors may make concessions. Those concessions may put limits on a defendant's exposure to sanctions.

Every case is different, and defendants should work closely with competent legal counsel when making decisions. Defendants should also do everything within their power to understand the system and all that follows after a criminal conviction.

When a defendant educates himself on how the system operates, he qualifies himself to make decisions from a position of strength. Too many people that come into the criminal justice system fail to understand the opportunity costs that come with every decision, including the length of time that passes before a guilty plea.

When hiring counsel, its crucial to be honest to save time and to help the attorney quarterback decisions. But hiring an attorney does not absolve the defendant from investing time and energy to learn more about:

» Strategies to prepare for sentencing,

» Doing the work to preparing for sentencing,

» Understanding sanctions that may follow sentencing,

» Preparing for a journey through the prison system,

» Preparing for the earliest possible release from prison,

» Understanding how to get best outcomes after prison

In subsequent chapters, we will offer insight defendants may consider on those subjects. The next chapter will offer thoughts to consider for those who need to find a criminal defense lawyer.

Chapter 3

How to Find a Lawyer

When I needed to find a criminal defense lawyer, I was a stockbroker. I'd never been in trouble before and I didn't have any idea where to turn. In my book, *Lessons from Prison,* I tell the story about all of the bad decisions that I made. By not understanding how to hire a lawyer, I flushed tens of thousands down the drain. Then, by not being honest with the lawyer during our initial meetings, I put myself in a worse position, exposing me to a significantly harsher punishment.

Through our consulting practice, our team interacts with thousands of people that face challenges with civil and criminal law enforcement agencies. While searching for information, they find the abundance of content we make available at either WhiteCollarAdvice.com, PrisonProfessors.com, or ResilienceCourses.com. We interact with many people that face potential charges.

Through our service, people frequently ask us for advice on how to find criminal defense lawyers. Perhaps a story about Darren, one of our clients, may illustrate the challenge people have.

Hiring a Lawyer:

Darren had been in business for more than a decade and he worked with corporate lawyers extensively. He contacted our team when he realized that some of his decisions on the job were about to expose him to problems with regulatory agencies, and possibly to challenges with the Department of Justice.

Darren's problem reminded me of my own challenges. As I wrote in *Lessons from Prison,* I was a stockbroker at UBS when I learned that some of my decisions brought me to the attention of officials at the Securities and Exchange Commission.

I knew that I needed a lawyer, but I didn't know how to find a lawyer.

When authorities like the SEC, the FCC, the FTC, or the FDA start asking questions about an individual, it's always best to find a lawyer. Darren had the right instinct to research steps he could take before hiring anyone.

By the time we spoke, Darren had already spent a lot of time on our website. Since he could identify with my background, he reached out. He asked how I went about finding a lawyer to represent me. I told him the truth: an acquaintance told me to hire a lawyer from the Jones Day law firm.

"I've heard of Jones Day," Darren said. "They're supposed to be great. How did it work out?"

Darren is right. The lawyers at Jones Day are some of the best litigators in the world. With more than 2,500 lawyers that practice across the US, Europe, and Asia, Jones Day has a strong reputation. But there is a cost that comes with hiring a firm of Jones Day's caliber.

Their lawyers command some of the highest fees in the legal profession. As I recall, I paid $50,000 to get in the door, not knowing whether they could help me or not. They exhausted those resources within the first three weeks.

I would've liked to have known more about legal billing when I went in. As a result of hiring Jones Day without a full understanding of the costs, I put myself at a huge disadvantage. That decision cost me both time and money.

At first, the cost upset me. Then I realized, I'm the one that didn't know how to find a lawyer. And as a result of my ignorance, I made a costly mistake.

When I realized that I couldn't afford to pay a mid-six-figure legal fee, I had to let Jones Day go. Then I went back into the marketplace to start over with a different lawyer. Again, I would have to pay to bring the lawyer up to speed.

Finding a lawyer is easy, I told Darren. Finding the *right* lawyer is another matter.

I told Darren about another client of mine, Jim, that used Google to find the lawyer he hired. The search pulled up an endless list of lawyers. Each of them had well-designed websites that touted their expertise.

"I didn't know what to expect, or how to hire a lawyer," Jim told me.

Jim scheduled an appointment with the first lawyer on the list. The lawyer listened to Jim's description of the problem. "Based on what you're telling me," the lawyer told Jim, "I think I can keep you out of prison."

That statement was exactly what Jim wanted to hear. But it wasn't what Jim needed to hear. Nevertheless, by pledging that he thought he could keep Jim from going to prison, Jim agreed to sign a retainer agreement. Then Jim provided the lawyer with a cashier's check for $50,000. The agreement indicated that Jim was required to keep $50,000 in the lawyer's trust account at all times. The lawyer would bill at the rate of $800 per hour.

At least Jim knew what he was paying. Or, I should say, he thought he knew.

The lawyer surprised Jim on his next visit. After reviewing Jim's case, the lawyer said he wanted Jim to hire a second lawyer. Further discussion led Jim to provide the second lawyer with an additional $50,000 retainer, and the second lawyer would also bill at the rate of $800 per hour.

When Jim sat in meetings, both lawyers would be present. Jim didn't realize he was paying $1,600 per hour to help the lawyers understand complexities of his case. He felt as if the first lawyer had misrepresented himself in order to get the case. Since Jim already invested $100,000, he felt he too far down the road to make a change.

Darren listened to my story and felt discouraged. If Jim didn't know how to find the right lawyer, and I didn't find the right lawyer, he didn't know how to proceed. He said that he had worked with several business lawyers over the course of his career.

"Wouldn't that be a good place to start?" I asked Darren. If he had a good relationship with business lawyers, they might be in a position to recommend a lawyer with the right type of experience to represent him on a potential criminal matter.

Darren could turn to those resources for help. He did not want them to know about his current predicament, or potential predicament. For that reason, he was doing his own research, which led him to my website at WhiteCollarAdvice.com.

We started working together and came up with a plan. Anyone could follow the same plan. Since Darren wanted to remain anonymous, at least for the time being, I did some preliminary work on his behalf. I wanted to filter prospective candidates that might agree to work on his behalf.

Use Contacts:

Since Darren couldn't reach out to his contacts, I decided to reach out to mine. I called:

- David Rosenfield, of Herrick Feinstein in New York.
- Mark Werksman, of Werksman, Jackson, and Quinn, in Los Angeles,
- David Willingham, of Boies Schiller Flexner, in Los Angeles, and
- Tom Warren, of Pierce Bainbridge.

Our team has had extensive experience working with those four lawyers. Like all of the lawyers with whom we've worked, we have enormous respect for them. They've proven to be trustworthy and responsive to communications, which is important to any defendant.

Since Darren was from Detroit, I told the lawyers that I was helping him find a lawyer in his jurisdiction. Although lawyers have the capacity to work in different jurisdictions, defendants should recognize that there are costs associated with making such arrangements. When hiring a lawyer from a different jurisdiction, the out-of-state lawyer must coordinate with a lawyer that is already licensed to practice in the jurisdiction. Generally, there is a fee for providing this service. The client would have to pay this fee. In addition, when a lawyer travels to different jurisdictions, the client will pay for those travel fees.

Further, there be an intangible value in hiring a local lawyer that has good working relationships with prosecutors and judges.

Darren wanted to preserve costs, so I asked our contacts to connect me with competent lawyers from the Detroit area that practiced in the area of law that would help Darren.

Any defendant searching to find a lawyer may want to research the lawyer's area of expertise. If a lawyer has extensive experience in a given area, that lawyer may be more familiar with case law, statutes, arguments, and decisions that could prove beneficial.

Within a few hours of reaching, we had a list of 10 lawyers in Detroit that people we trusted recommended. Each lawyer on the list had specific experience with the specific type of case that Darren could potentially face.

I made initial contact with an email, explaining that I was vetting lawyers. That research helped me to start filtering. By asking questions, I learned:

» About each lawyer's rate for billable hours,
    - Important to know so a defendant can get an idea of how much to budget. In some cases, a lawyer may be able to resolve a plea negotiation and guilty plea in less than 100 billable hours, preparing for trial in federal court would likely require several hundred billable hours.

- » About the lawyer's position on accepting a flat fee for the entire case,
    - o A flat fee may or may not serve the interest of the defendant. Every case is different. On the plus side, a defendant that has a flat fee knows exactly how much to budget. On the negative side, a lawyer that receives a flat fee may be disinclined to devote much time to the case after he is paid.
- » About the types of cases he or she practiced,
    - o A lawyer that specializes in defending tax cases may not be the best fit for a defendant facing criminal charges related to mail fraud that could result in the loss of liberty.
- » About the lawyer's expertise in sentencing matters,
    - o More than 75 percent of the people that face charges in federal court eventually have a sentencing hearing. What level of expertise does the prospective lawyer have with sentencing in the given jurisdiction?
- » About the size of the lawyer's team,
    - o A lawyer with a large team may be able to outsource work to associates or paralegals that bill at a lower hourly rate. The lawyer will have discretion, but it's helpful to know that the lawyer is cost-conscious of a defendant's resources.

- » About the lawyer's philosophy on communication with clients,
    - o Some lawyers make themselves readily available to defendants, even providing cell-phone numbers for communication. Other lawyers prefer to work independently, leaving defendants out of the communication loop.
- » About whether the lawyer would be receptive to accepting a 5-hour retainer to get started, just to see if a good fit exists for a productive working relationship.
    - o Some lawyers will not get started on a case without a minimum retainer. In federal cases, that initial retainer often exceeds $50,000. As Jim experienced, it's difficult to make an assessment on an initial free consultation.

That model proved worthwhile for Darren. John Dakmak, a senior lawyer with Clark Hill, in Detroit, agreed to take an initial retainer for a few hours of work. John was able to make some phone calls and give Darren a better sense of where things stood in the investigation. The relationship has served Darren extremely well. Despite an investigation that has lasted for several years, Darren reports that Mr. Dakmak has always been responsive. He offers a glowing endorsement for the representation he has received.

If you're searching to find a lawyer, create a plan.

To the extent that it's possible, create a series of questions that will help you gauge whether the attorney is the right fit for you. It's important to be honest about your current situation and what you expect.

If you go into a meeting with a lawyer and minimize your conduct, you may set yourself up for a bad outcome.

Brian, for example, was a director with a large financial services company. His employer had an insurance policy for "officers and directors." The policy would pay legal fees for people in specific positions. When federal authorities indicted Brian, he hired an experienced white-collar criminal defense attorney that would send all bills to the insurance company. The law firm launched a scorched-earth defense strategy, and quickly burned through the $500,000 cap on legal fees. When that insurance bill expired, the lawyers told Brian that he should plead guilty and that he would be responsible for the remainder of his bill—which amounted to an additional $75,000.

"I always knew that at the end of the day, I was going to plead guilty," Brian told me. "When I went to find a lawyer, I went along with what they said. They wanted to contest every document. But every time they read a document, they charged exorbitant fees. There bills showed that I was burning through more than $20,000 on legal fees some days."

If it's true that Brian knew he would eventually plead guilty, when he looked to find a lawyer, he may have been better suited to find an attorney with a strong track record of making great plea deals.

At the end of the day, any defendant that needs to learn how to find a lawyer should follow the path that Darren pursued.

To the extent possible, use contacts to ascertain the expertise, honesty, and competence of lawyers with regard to specific types of cases, in a specific jurisdiction.

Approach those lawyers with a list of questions that will help you determine if you think that you work well together. To the extent possible, ask the lawyer to accept a limited engagement to test the waters. Most importantly, make certain that you have the financial resources available to support the decision you make.

Chapter 4

What are Criminal Justice Proceedings?

Hopefully, once you find and hire a lawyer, you'll have a trusted advocate.

When it comes to criminal matters, unfortunately, finding and hiring a criminal-defense attorney is only the start of a long and arduous path. The more a defendant learns about the challenges ahead, and the better he understands how he can prepare, the more likely he will be to conquer struggles that complicate life for so many that experience the criminal justice system.

I don't have precise statistics in front of me. Still, I don't think anyone will argue that if federal prosecutors bring criminal charges against individuals, a sentencing hearing will follow more than six out of ten times. Before banging the gavel to signal finality, the judge frequently says:

» "I sentence you to the custody of the Attorney General."

Several years ago, a federal judge in the Southern District of California invited our team to lead a panel discussion for other judges in his district. They wanted us to help judges understand what happens after they sentence a person to prison.

If federal judges don't know what happens after they sentence a person, it's fair to say that neither lawyers nor defendants know what to expect either. In fact, some defendants don't even know how they got into the system.

How does it Start:

Relatively few Americans have more than a basic understanding of our nation's criminal justice system. They know that law enforcement officers arrest people, district attorneys prosecute many of those who are arrested, and some people who are convicted go to jail or prison. It's much more complicated than that, of course.

Although I'm not a lawyer, I've done a lot of research to get a better understanding of the system, and I found an excellent resource in *Modern Criminal Procedure, 9th Edition*, by Yale Kamisar, et al, published by West Group, (St. Paul. Minn: 1999). It's a great resource for anyone that wants to get a more thorough understanding of the system.

Most people don't need to read a legal treatise. The summary I provide below will give most defendants a better understanding of how the criminal justice machine works. That understanding may lead to more fluency, better communications, and better preparation for the journey ahead.

Again, we're writing for laymen, for people who want a brief glimpse of what to expect if charged with a felony.

Start from the premise that our criminal justice system is designed to protect society. It doesn't always seem that way for a defendant. When a defendant comes into the system, everything feels like a personal attack, and the complicated proceedings aren't always easy to understand.

Lawyers talk about substantive laws (the laws that congress passed) and about proceedings (the rules by which the system is supposed to operate). It isn't a perfect system, because it has evolved over multiple decades, and it's designed to operate at scale. A system designed to process more than 1 million people each year doesn't look too closely at personal characteristics and circumstances. It's much more like moving a cog through an elaborate machine.

All branches of law enforcement work together to prosecute crimes. Just as some offenders will make every effort to evade detection and apprehension by law-enforcement officers, representatives of the criminal justice system will make every effort to convict a defendant.

Many defendants complain that law enforcement officers and prosecutors operate outside the scope of the rules in order to get convictions. Unfortunately, complaining doesn't solve any problems. Once a person comes into the system, it's best to think methodically. We need to learn as much as possible, and then engineer our way to the best outcome.

Throughout this book and course, we'll offer insight that defendants may use—along with their counsel—to prepare.

Practically speaking, defendants would be well advised to *expect* law enforcement officers and prosecutors to use every means available for them to achieve their ends. Ultimately, prosecutors want to solve crimes and convict. In a perfect world those representatives of justice would dot every "I" and cross every "T" as they follow the rules in both the letter and the spirit of the law.

Years of working with society's felons, however, frequently causes seasoned law enforcement officers to develop cynical perspectives of humanity. Sometimes, to get the outcome they want, they cut corners. They may even threaten. Let me give an example from a client that our team is working with now.

Sam is a healthcare professional. The prosecutor offered him an opportunity to plead guilty to a charge with a five-year cap. If Sam chose to exercise his right to a jury trial, the prosecutor threatened to bring charges against Sam's wife, and to bring further charges that would expose Sam to more than 20 years in prison. Then, the prosecutor argued that Sam would have to agree to say that no one pressured, threatened, or induced him to take the plea.

From Sam's perspective, the proceeding is inherently unfair. He would like to have had an opportunity to argue for his innocence. But he could not afford to expose his wife to the threat of criminal charges. He felt threatened and pressured to take the deal. Rather than justice, Sam said the prosecutor wanted a conviction.

Those who work in law enforcement tend to become ultra conservative. They may be rigid in their beliefs that people who are charged with crimes clearly did something wrong and ought to be punished. Such attitudes can result in offenders being charged with crimes that can result in convictions, as opposed to the offender being charged with precisely the crimes that the individual may have actually committed.

It would be wise, I think, for those who become entangled with the criminal justice process to anticipate a system influenced much more by Machiavelli, pursuing victory regardless of methods, rather than a system influenced by teachings of more enlightened leaders that encourage forgiveness, compassion, and concern for the individual.

The Structure:

In compliance with our nation's Constitution, legislators elected to both houses of the U.S. Congress have played a significant role in establishing a body of federal laws that are supposed to govern the behavior of citizens.

The Constitution also provides legislators from each individual state with authority to establish their own code of criminal laws for their state, and their own criminal justice processes for enforcing those laws statewide. Although the different jurisdictions frequently collaborate, our nation actually operates several different criminal justice systems:

» We have a system for the federal government,

» We have a system for each state,

» We have a system for the military, and

» We have another system for the District of Columbia.

It's our responsibility as citizens to abide by these laws. When we do not, we subject ourselves to being charged with criminal offenses and experiencing the wrath of the criminal justice system.

Law enforcement officers are supposed to follow strictly prescribed procedures when charging a citizen with wrongdoing. In addition to federal and state rules for criminal procedure, published judicial opinions may also have an impact on criminal procedures.

Criminal procedures are complicated. They can be understood more easily when we think of the criminal justice system as a game. I use this metaphor for clarity, not to trivialize the conflict between accused and accuser.

Offenders, or "defendants" act as opponents of law enforcement officers and prosecutors. Both sides want to win. The defendants want to be acquitted, or to receive the least restrictive sanction.

On the other side, law enforcement officers and prosecutors want to convict. They frequently argue for defendants to receive severe sanctions, without consideration for individual characteristics or mitigating factors. A judge will make the ultimate decision.

In this "game" of criminal justice, the judge acts as referee. Judges are charged with the responsibility of ensuring that all participants of the game follow procedures to ensure that *due process* is achieved. Although there are many ways this game may begin, it usually starts when someone reports a crime to a member of law enforcement.

Once the Crime is Reported:

The criminal justice process usually begins when a crime is reported or otherwise discovered by law enforcement officers. Law enforcement officers may learn about a crime in any number of ways.

» They may observe a crime being committed;

» They may learn about it because someone reports it;

» They may learn about it through investigation or by interrogating others.

Once law enforcement officers learn about a crime, it becomes a "reported crime" or a "known offense."

Pre-Arrest Investigation

Sometimes, as when law enforcement officers are present when a crime is being committed—or soon thereafter—the "investigation" begins with an *on-scene arrest*. Other times, as when law enforcement officers learn that a crime has been committed, but were not in a position to make an on-scene arrest, they have the responsibility of solving that crime.

They therefore launch a *reactive investigation*, where the officers will attempt to figure out:

» Whether a crime was in fact committed,

» Who committed the crime,

» What evidence there is of guilt, and

» How to locate the offender to make an arrest.

Proactive investigations, on the other hand, are aimed to solve crimes that are ongoing or that may take place in the future. These types of investigations place law enforcement officers in a position to uncover criminal activity, the specifics of which are not known, or where they do not have enough information to charge all whom may be participants in the crime.

Another type of pre-arrest investigation includes the *prosecutorial investigation*, which is generally conducted by a prosecutor. The prosecutor has the power to convene a grand jury (see below for discussion on the grand jury) and, through the power of the grand jury issue a subpoena.

Individuals who receive such a subpoena must appear before the grand jury and answer questions that the prosecutor poses in the criminal investigation.

Since the person who received the subpoena does not have counsel present during the questioning, and the entire grand jury proceeding is orchestrated by a prosecutor, it has become routine for grand juries to rubber stamp the recommendations of the prosecutor.

Arrest:

An arrest, of course, is when the law enforcement officer takes a person into custody. Sometimes, the arrest occurs at the scene of a crime. In cases that evolved from reactive or proactive investigations, on the other hand, the officers will obtain an arrest warrant—usually from a magistrate judge—before taking the person into custody.

In some cases, officers will allow the suspect to turn himself in. In other cases, law enforcement officers will make a spectacle. In those cases, the officers use an extreme show of force—frequently with weapons drawn—at an inconvenient time, like the break of dawn or during a person's work hours.

Booking:

If the person was arrested publicly, the officers will search him. They may search his vehicle, home, or office. They're looking for contraband, weapons, or evidence of a crime. Then they transport the suspect to a jail, a courthouse, or some other type of holding facility for further processing, or "booking."

During the booking procedure, the officers will conduct clerical procedures to memorialize the arrest. They record fingerprints and photograph the suspect (the well-known mug shots). If it's a minor crime, authorities may release the suspect from the holding facility.

If the alleged crime is more serious in nature, authorities may hold the suspect for several hours, or even days, until he can appear before a judge who will determine whether bail is appropriate. If the offender is held in lockup, it is likely that he will be ordered to undergo a strip search.

Post-Arrest investigation:

Immediately after the arrest, the post-arrest investigation begins. The first step is when the officers search the person—and possibly his vehicle, home, or office—for evidence that can be used against him.

After that, law enforcement officers may conclude that little else needs to be done (in the event that they caught the suspect in the act), or they may continue with many of the same types of techniques used in reactive and proactive investigations, such as interviews and searches.

Deciding to Charge:

When law enforcement officers witness a crime, they make a decision on whether to charge the suspected offender. Then, after the individual has been processed through booking, superior officers may review the arrest and decide whether to allow it to proceed. If the law enforcement agency chooses to proceed with prosecution, the prosecutors will then review the charge.

The prosecutor may interview the arresting officer and review the evidence to determine whether the case is worthy of a filing of the criminal charge. Reasons why a prosecutor may decline to file charges include:

» Insufficient evidence;

» Witness difficulties;

» Due process problems;

» Alternatives to prosecution; and

» Diversion programs that enable the suspect to avoid a criminal record.

Even if the prosecutor initially chooses to charge an individual, he may change his decision. Later, he may determine that the charge is not justified or that a lesser charge is more appropriate. In those cases, the prosecutor would have to file a motion before the court detailing the prosecutor's reasons to forego prosecution. The prosecutor would use the same screening factors identified above to determine the appropriateness of such a motion.

Filing the Complaint:

In many cases, if the charges pass the prosecutor's screening, the next step will come when the prosecutor files the complaint, most likely with a magistrate judge. The complaint is usually a fairly brief document, concisely detailing the criminal allegations.

When a complaint is used as the charging instrument, someone must sign the complaint under oath indicating that he or she believes the factual allegations of the complaint to be true. Usually it's the victim or the investigating officer who signs the complaint. With the filing of the complaint, the suspect officially becomes a defendant in a criminal proceeding.

Review of the Arrest by Magistrate:

Many jurisdictions appoint magistrate judges to take some of the workload away from trial judges. Among other things, the magistrate judges handle many of the pre-trial matters.

After the prosecutor files the complaint with the court, but before the defendant's first appearance, for example, it frequently will be a magistrate judge who reviews the charges against the defendant.

If the defendant was arrested without a warrant and remains in custody, the magistrate must determine whether probable cause exists for the defendant's continued detention. In the extremely rare instance that the judge finds that the prosecutor has not established probable cause, the prosecution either must produce more information or release the arrested person.

First Appearance:

With the filing of the complaint, the defendant is brought before the judge "without unnecessary delay." Several hours or several days may pass before the defendant sees a judge, depending on the circumstances.

If a defendant is arrested late on a Friday afternoon, he may not see the judge until the following Monday.

The first appearance is generally a brief proceeding in which the magistrate determines that the person named on the complaint is the person before the court. After the magistrate is convinced that the appropriate person is present, the judge will read the charges made against the defendant, identify the defendant's rights, and in felony cases, advise the defendant of the next step in the process, which is the preliminary hearing.

The magistrate then sets a date for the preliminary hearing, which the defendant may choose to waive. The magistrate judge then will ask the defendant to enter a plea; if the defendant pleads not guilty, the judge will set a trial date.

Defendants are entitled to have counsel present at every stage of all felony criminal justice proceedings. If the individual cannot afford counsel, the court will provide a court-appointed attorney.

A substantial percentage of all felony defendants go through their criminal justice proceedings with court-appointed counsel. These attorneys may work for a public defender service, or they may be in private practice but make themselves available to represent a limited number of indigent defendants. As a practical matter, the indigent defendants who use court-appointed counsel do not have much choice as to which attorney represents them.

Bail:

If the defendant is in custody at the time of his first appearance, one of the most important functions of the proceeding is for the magistrate judge to determine whether bail is appropriate. Bail establishes the conditions under which the defendant can be released from confinement until his case is decided.

If the magistrate judge agrees that bail is warranted in the case, he may require the defendant to post bail in cash, with a surety bond, or by signing over a deed to property. The judge also may accept the defendant's personal guarantee that he will present himself for trial.

In general, the magistrate is expected to impose such bail conditions as appear reasonably necessary to assure that the defendant will make court appearances as scheduled throughout the criminal justice proceedings.

There is a presumption that a defendant is entitled to bail. Unfortunately, in drug cases or other serious offenses, judges refuse to release a defendant on bail. The magistrate generally looks to the seriousness of the crime, the defendant's criminal history, the defendant's risk of flight, and the defendant's ties to the community when deliberating over the appropriate bail conditions.

Preliminary Hearing:

After the first appearance, the next scheduled step is the preliminary hearing. Defendants who choose to plead guilty frequently waive the preliminary hearing. Some jurisdictions allow the prosecutor to bypass the preliminary hearing, which is yet another screening of the charge, by immediately obtaining a grand jury indictment.

In jurisdictions that allow preliminary hearings, magistrate judge presides over this first step. Since this phase of the process is adversarial in nature, the defendant should have counsel present to represent him.

Generally, during this proceeding, the prosecutor will provide witnesses and the defendant's counsel will have the opportunity to cross-examine. After listening to the proceeding, the magistrate judge will determine whether to advance the case to the next level—which either is a grand jury review or the filing of a criminal information or complaint.

Grand Jury Review:

In the federal system, all felony prosecutions require a grand jury review. The only exception is when the defendant waives this review and agrees to be charged with a criminal complaint or information.

States vary in their requirements for charges. The primary function of the grand jury review is to determine whether sufficient evidence exists to proceed with a trial on the criminal charges. A number of randomly chosen citizens sit on the grand jury panel, usually between 12 and 23. Those grand jurors listen as the prosecution presents its case. The prosecution uses its subpoena power to call witnesses before the grand jury, then questions those witnesses under oath.

Witnesses do not have the right to legal counsel during the grand jury proceeding, and there is no cross-examination. Accordingly, the proceeding is really a one-sided show for the prosecution.

When the prosecution does persuade the grand jury that there is merit to the criminal charge, the grand jury returns an indictment. Although the grand jury is said to be a screening device, many in the legal profession ridicule it.

Since defendants can't speak on their own behalf, and targets may not even know that a prosecutor convened a grand jury, prosecutors have their way. They get to build arguments without giving the target an opportunity to respond. For that reason, experts say a prosecutor could use a grand jury to indict a ham sandwich.

When a grand jury does issue an indictment, that document is filed with the trial court, replacing the original complaint or accusatory instrument in the case. If a grand jury review was not sought, either because it was not required or it was waived, the prosecutor simply would file the criminal complaint or information with the trial court.

The Arraignment:

After the accusatory instrument is filed with the trial court, the defendant is brought before the trial court to be informed of the charges against him. The trial court judge will ask the defendant how he pleads. Ordinarily, the options for the defendant are to plead guilty or not guilty.

This procedure is known as arraigning the defendant. In most cases, defendants plead not guilty at the earliest stages. This strategy gives the defendant more time to examine the strength of the government's case. It also allows time for the possible negotiation of more favorable conditions under which the defendant will agree to plead guilty—as most defendants eventually do.

Plea Bargaining and Proffers:

Prosecutors want defendants to plead guilty. Ultimately, they want a conviction. Trials require substantial amounts of government time and resources. Further, the outcome of a trial is uncertain.

Accordingly, prosecutors frequently grant concessions to induce defendants to plead guilty. For example, they may agree to dismiss certain charges, or they may agree not to prosecute a family member.

Prosecutors want to avoid the time and expense of a trial. They may invite a defendant to proffer what he would show through trial, or the prosecutorial team may proffer what it could prove during a trial. All of those negotiations are designed to come to an agreement that would avoid a trial.

This procedure is frequently called plea bargaining. The prosecutor has the authority to charge a defendant with crimes that carry certain sentences. They also have the ability to recommend certain sentences within the statute or guideline range.

In the end, the judge imposes a sentence. Although the judge may listen to the prosecutor's sentencing recommendation, prosecutors do not have the power to bind a judge's decision.

The vast majority of defendants enter guilty pleas. Frequently, defendants that plead guilty spend much of their time in prison second-guessing their decision. Experience convinces us that defendants who know they are guilty are vastly better off:

» To accept complete responsibility,

» To express remorse,

» To plead guilty at the earliest possible stage, and

» To work toward an effective sentence-mitigation strategy.

Like all decisions where liberty is at stake, deciding whether to plead guilty is a legal decision that must be made with the guidance of counsel.

Pre-Trial Motions:

After the arraignment, attorneys for the defendant may choose to file multiple pretrial motions before the trial court in an effort to help them develop a better understanding of the government's evidence. These motions may:

» Attack the charging instrument—either the criminal information or the grand jury process;

» Ask for an order directing the government to disclose evidence;

» Request the court to suppress evidence that the defendant believes was obtained in violation of the defendant's Constitutional rights.

The Trial

If the case has not been dismissed, and the defendant has not pled guilty, the next step in the criminal justice procedure is the trial. Defendants have a right to a speedy trial, but the defendant may waive that right. The prosecutor may look for excusable opportunities to extend the pretrial time period.

Both sides of the adversarial process look for every opportunity to prepare their case. In a typical jurisdiction, it is reasonable to expect five to ten months to pass from the time of arrest until the time the trial begins. Some trials may require only a few hours, others several weeks. Complicated cases may stretch into several months—or even years—before both sides present their closing arguments.

Although some defendants choose a bench trial, with only a judge to determine one's guilt or innocence, all felony defendants have the right to a jury trial. In a jury trial, a group of randomly selected citizens is charged with the responsibility of listening to the evidence that the trial judge allows to be presented.

The jurors are supposed to presume that the defendant is not guilty of the charges until the trial judge instructs them to begin deliberating on whether the prosecution has proven its case.

The trial begins with the voir dire process, which is the questioning of jurors. The judge, and in some jurisdictions the attorneys play a role in questioning the prospective jurors. During voir dire, both the defense and prosecution will try to filter prospective jurors that may be biased against their side.

The theory may hold that both sides are seeking justice. In reality, the prosecution is seeking a conviction and the defendant is seeking an acquittal. Each side is looking for the best group of jurors to deliver the desired verdict. The judge will determine how many prospective jurors each lawyer can remove from the potential jury.

Once the jury has been chosen and sworn, the prosecution and the defense may begin with an opening argument. After opening arguments, the prosecution will begin presenting its case, usually with live witnesses whom the defense may then cross-examine.

After the prosecution rests, the defense will have an opportunity to present its case and the prosecutor can cross-examine its witnesses. Then, after both sides have rested, the prosecutor will make a closing argument. The defendant's attorney will have an opportunity to make a closing argument. The prosecutor gets the last word, though, in response to the defense attorney's closing argument.

Finally, the judge will read a set of instructions to the jury. Once the judge releases the jury to the jury room, members are supposed to start considering all of the evidence as they deliberate on whether the prosecution has proven its case.

To obtain a conviction, each member of the jury must find the defendant guilty beyond a reasonable doubt. Once the jury reaches a verdict, and it's announced in court, the judge concludes the trial.

If it's a guilty verdict, whether after a trial or as a result of a plea, a series of post-conviction proceedings will follow. In the next chapter, we'll offer insight on post-conviction proceedings in the criminal justice system.

Chapter 5

What Are Post-Conviction Proceedings?

In the United States, we like to say that a person is presumed innocent until there has been a finding of guilt. Defendants don't always feel that presumption of guilt. A criminal charge may result in being ostracized by friends, loss of employment, and even loss of housing. Those collateral consequences make a difficult situation worse.

From a legal perspective, life officially changes after a conviction. Prior to the conviction, the defendant may have gone through a "pre-trial services" program. While in the "pre-trial phase," a judicial employee or probation officer may lightly oversee the defendant, imposing light restrictions. As an example, rules may require a person in the pre-trial phase to request permission before traveling outside of a specific jurisdiction.

With a criminal conviction, more formal proceedings will follow. For felony cases, a pre-sentence investigation and ensuing report will follow the conviction.

Pre-Sentence Investigation Report (PSI or PSR—used interchangeably):

Once a defendant pleads guilty, or a jury convicts the defendant, the person becomes a convicted felon.

In most felony cases, the court will order the probation department to conduct a pre-sentence investigation. This investigation will result in a report that has a lasting influence on the defendant's life.

The pre-sentence investigation report provides about the person's background for the sentencing judge, staff members in the prison system, and the probation officer that will supervisor the person after release. Essentially, the report will begin with a narration of the prosecution's version of the offense. The probation officer will interview the defendant and give him an opportunity to make a statement, too.

Besides interviewing the defendant, the probation officer will conduct an investigation into the defendant's personal background. It is not uncommon for the probation officer conducting the report to speak with the defendant's family members, friends, employers, and anyone else that may provide material information.

Major cases will result in more extensive pre-sentence investigations to provide the judge (and others) with a snapshot of the offense and the defendant's background. The judge relies on this information as a source of reference when deliberating over the appropriate sanction to impose.

Those going to prison should not underestimate the importance of the PSR. The PSR will have a big influence on the person while he is in prison and while he is on Supervised Release. Because of the PSR's importance, we devote chapter seven to the process, revealing how our team works with clients that choose to prepare before their interview with the probation officer.

Sentencing:

After the finding of guilt, and the completion of the PSR, the next step in the criminal justice process is sentencing. In most cases, sentencing is a function of the court. Basically, the sentencing judge has three alternatives:

» For the most serious crimes, the sentencing judge may impose a term of imprisonment.

» For crimes that the judge deems less severe, the judge may impose a term of probation, allowing the offender to remain in the community under specific conditions.

» Or, the judge may impose some type of financial sanction, like a fine or restitution.

Generally, the legislature determined the range of sanctions from which the judge can choose.

For federal crimes, judges must rely upon the sentencing guidelines when determining what sentence to impose. The guidelines are not "mandatory," but judges must consider them. As a result of a Supreme Court case, judges must consider personal characteristics. Those characteristics may warrant a sentence either below or above the guideline range. For that reason, our team recommends that defendants consider a multipronged approach to prepare prior to sentencing.

Congress designed the guidelines to create uniformity in sentencing. They provide a matrix that take many dynamics into consideration. Among other factors, guidelines consider the defendant's role in the offense, the defendant's acceptance of responsibility, aggravating factors, mitigating factors, and the defendant's criminal history. The Federal Sentencing Guidelines Manual provides details that judges may consider as they deliberate over appropriate sanctions.

Anyone anticipating the possibility of receiving a federal sentence ought to read guidelines manual to understand more about what judges consider when sentencing a defendant. Our team has interviewed several federal judges. They've given us insight with regard to steps a defendant should take in anticipation of sentencing. Specifically, judges want to know:

» What does the defendant understand about victims in the case?

» What led the defendant into the criminal behavior?

» What has the defendant learned from the process?

» What steps has the defendant taken to reconcile with society?

Although the defendant's attorney will prepare legal arguments to advocate for the defendant, every defendant should work to advocate for himself. Our team urges defendants to work toward a multi-part strategy that includes:

1. Preparing a sentencing narrative.
2. Preparing a sentencing video.
3. Preparing a package of character-reference letters.
4. Preparing a sentence-mitigation story of reconciliation with society.

Our catalog offers details on each of those options. This multi-part strategy will help the judge get to know the defendant's true nature. It can lead to mercy, or the least restrictive sanction. Read more about these options by texting the following word, to the following number:

- » Text number: 44222
- » Test following word: ***Sentence***
- » Or visit ResilientCourses.com

If the defendant has been out on a bond, the judge may order the defendant into custody after the sentencing hearing. In other cases, the judge authorizes the defendant to report to prison later. Our team has seen cases with different outcomes. If the defendant makes a credible argument, he may have reason to wait several months before surrendering to prison. In the rarest of circumstances, defendants may remain free on bond pending the outcome of an appeal.

Every case is unique. Defendants should consider the pros and the cons of prolonging a surrender date to prison. In some cases, it makes sense to get to prison at the soonest possible time. In other cases, valid reasons exist to postpone the surrender date.

Becoming a Prisoner / Good Time / Earned Time:

After the judge sentences a person, a transition takes place. In the federal system, the trial judge loses jurisdiction over the case in a matter of days. The U.S. Marshal Service sends the Judgment Order, along with the PSR, to the administrative office of the Bureau of Prisons, in Grand Prairie, Texas. Prison staff members then rely upon a program statement, known as the Custody and Classification Manual. That manual includes a scoring system that results in a "security-level" score and a "custody-level" score. BOP officials in Grand Prairie rely upon those scores and other factors to determine where the prisoner will serve the sentence.

In December of 2018, President Trump signed the First Step Act. The First Step Act is the most significant criminal-justice reform legislation in more than two decades.

Although the president signed the law, as of early summer 2019, the Bureau of Prisons has not yet fully implemented the First Step Act.

We do not anticipate people in prison getting the full benefit of the law until 2020. As more details become available, we will update this book and our courses on ResilientCourses.com. For more current information on details of The First Step Act, please visit our websites at:

» PrisonProfessors.com, or

» WhiteCollarAdvice.com

Every person in federal prison will benefit from this new law. For example, as a result of the legislation, people in federal prison will receive a full 15 percent reduction in their sentences if they abide by rules in federal prison. Further, the law requires officials in the BOP to authorize more self-help programs for people in prison. Some examples of positive programs in federal prison include:

» Education courses
» Vocational courses
» Fitness courses
» Spiritual-development courses
» Substance-abuse treatment programs

All prisoners that remain active in those positive programs will derive some form of benefit from participating. But if the Bureau of Prisons officials determine that the qualified prisoners are at "low- or minimal-risk" of recidivating, those prisoners will receive "Earned Time" credits of 15 days each month.

It's important to differentiate "Good Time" credits from "Earned Time" credits. Prisoners receive up to 54 days each year in Good Time credits if they avoid being charged with any disciplinary conduct. Prisoners don't have to do anything particularly good to get the Good Time. They simply must avoid doing anything bad. By adhering to rules, a prisoner's sentence will be cut by 54 days per year.

The First Step Act does not cut time that a prisoner owes to complete the sentence. Rather, the prisoner that works to develop skills through good behavior and positive programming accumulates Earned Time credits at a rate of either 10-days per month, or 15-days per month.

At the end of the sentence, the *qualifying* prisoner will be able to rely upon those Earned Time credits as an objective mechanism to transition into home confinement earlier than would otherwise be possible. Qualifying prisoners may serve significant lengths of time on home confinement.

For example, let's say a person qualifies for the maximum benefit under the First Step Act. That person may have a federal conviction and he may have received a sentence of 100 months. That person may qualify for the Residential Drug Abuse Program, too.

The table below offers an estimate on what he could expect to serve with and without the First Step Act.

Factor	With First Step Act	Without First Step Act
100-Month Sentence	100-Month Sentence	100-Month Sentence
Good Time Credits	15% of sentence, which reduces sentence to 85 months.	15% of sentence, which reduces sentence to 85 months.
RDAP time reduction	12 months off sentence, which reduces sentence to 73 months.	12 months off sentence, which reduces sentence to 73 months.
Earned Time Credit at 15 days per month	Roughly 50% of time to Residential Reentry Center, resulting in transfer to home confinement at somewhere between 37 and 42 months.	Six to 12 months Residential Reentry Center, resulting in transfer to halfway house or home confinement at around 61 to 67 months.

Although the above table is only an estimate, and we won't have final details until the Bureau of Prisons releases its policy statement on the First Step Act, it's clear that this law will bring a positive benefit to many people in prison.

When it comes to Earned Time credits, the operative word is "qualifying" prisoner. Congress detailed a specific list of offenses that do not qualify for Earned Time credits. Generally speaking, people convicted of non-violent offenses qualify for Earned Time.

Again, we will update our sections on Earned Time as the Bureau of Prisons releases policy statements on this law.

Getting to Prison:

Once an individual is sentenced to prison, the next step is getting there. Offenders who are sentenced to relatively short terms, fewer than ten years, may have the privilege of surrendering to the facility to which they have been *designated* or assigned to serve their sentence.

The vast majority of people will be taken into custody and proceed through the humiliating prisoner transfer system. Future chapters will describe what to expect when being transferred to an initial prison, or from one prison to another.

Appeals and Post-Conviction Remedies:

Most defendants will enter into plea agreements that prohibit them from launching direct appeals. Prisoners that proceed through trial, on the other hand, routinely appeal if the jury convicted them. They may appeal errors in due process. In rare circumstances, such as if they discovered information that had not previously been available, they may appeal issues that the trial court did not consider. Otherwise, appellate courts review errors that the lower court may have made, which would have violated the defendant's due process rights.

Every step in the judicial proceeding brings the case one step closer to finality.

The U.S. Supreme Court, being the highest court in the land, is the court of last resort. Few defendants ever see their cases advance that far in the appellate procedure.

Indeed, relatively few offenders find any relief through appellate procedures. According to *Modern Criminal Procedure, 9th Edition*, by Yale Kamisar, et al, published by West Group, (St. Paul. Minn: 1999)—which we relied upon heavily to write this chapter—fewer than 11 percent of all defendants succeed on appeal.

Within one year after the appellate process is exhausted, those in prison may seek relief through habeas corpus, a civil (rather than criminal) proceeding. It is difficult to undo the long record that already has been established. The judicial concept of *stare decisis,* meaning "Let the decision stand" weighs heavily against defendants that seek relief through habeas corpus. Nevertheless, if defendants believe that their constitutional rights have been violated, such as if their attorney failed to represent them appropriately, and they file their motion within time limits authorized by the rules of civil procedure, they may attempt to get judicial relief through motions such as the §2255 motion.

Besides a defendant's motion, a prosecutor may initiate a post-conviction motion that gives jurisdiction back to the sentencing judge. As an example, prosecutors may file a Rule 35 motion. Prosecutors rely upon the Rule 35 as a tool to encourage people that have been sentenced to cooperate against others. By filing a Rule 35, prosecutors ask the judge to resentence the defendant to a lower term.

Final Word:

Anyone anticipating a potential problem with the criminal justice system should learn as much about the system as possible. The more knowledge a person has about the system, the better-prepared he will be to work with his attorney to achieve the best possible outcome.

People should rely on their attorneys for legal advice. Yet they also should make efforts to gather and learn from the experiences of others. Do not be an ostrich, living as though problems with the criminal justice system will somehow disappear.

If charged with a crime, we recommend reading the statute to find a complete definition of the elements of the offense. The defendant should read through potential penalties as well. The defendant does not have to speak with a law enforcement officer, but if he chooses to speak, he had better not lie. Lying to any law enforcement officer exposes the person to more problems—like obstruction of justice charges, or charges of making a false statement to a federal officer.

If ensnared in the criminal justice web, think about damage control. It's best to think proactively about navigating the challenges ahead. Learn the stakes associated with every decision.

When considering whether to go to trial or plead guilty, remember that sentencing guidelines incentivize those that expresses remorse and accept responsibility. The sooner a person starts preparing for leniency at sentencing, the better.

Although holding the prosecutor to task on every issue may bring some advantages, that option does not come without potential costs—both in terms of financial costs to launch an aggressive defense, and costs in terms of exposure to more difficult sanctions.

Chapter 6

What is a Sentence-Mitigation Plan?

When is the right time think about a sentence-mitigation plan?

Answering that question reminds me of an old saying about the best time to plant an oak tree. I heard a speaker ask that question to members of his audience. Predictably, audience members ventured a guess.

» In the morning?

» In the winter?

» In the summer?

No one had a clue.

Pausing for dramatic effect, the speaker then gave the answer. The best time to plant an oak tree was 20 years ago. The second-best time is today.

We could say the same thing about a sentence-mitigation plan. Too often, a defendant doesn't do anything to prepare for the sentencing hearing.

It's understandable. Many defendants don't think of themselves as criminals. Regardless of what type of activity brought them to the attention of authorities, they think that they're different, immune from law enforcement. They may not know anyone that has been through the criminal justice system, and they cannot conceive of themselves going into the system.

In my book, *Lessons from Prison*, I spoke about my experience. For several years, I worked as a stockbroker. I thought of myself as a professional in the financial services industry. When I learned that authorities were about to charge me with violating securities laws, I believed that I could maneuver my way out. In time, I believed that prosecutors would see me as I saw myself:

» A good son

» A college graduate

» A taxpayer

But authorities saw me differently. In their eyes, I violated securities laws. That made me a target for prosecution. And when federal authorities target a person for prosecution, their conviction rates exceed 85 percent. With those odds, it makes a lot of sense to begin thinking about a sentence-mitigation plan at the soonest possible time. Regardless of what type of charge a person faces, it's important to realize that sentencing proceedings will likely follow. Sentence-mitigation plans can help.

Start with an understanding of what the defense attorney will do. Attorneys will work with:

» The evidence against the individual,

» The procedural rules that determine what evidence the court will consider,

» The substantive law that Congress has passed,

» The case law that judges have decided,

» The prosecutor's ability to prove a case against the defendant.

To succeed, the defense attorney will exercise judgment and discretion, fighting valiantly to get the best possible outcome for the defendant. Both the prosecutor and the defense attorney will be analyzing the case and pressing forward to get the outcome they want. Rather than justice, the prosecutor will strive for a conviction. The defense attorney will parry the prosecutor's efforts, always assessing the strength of arguments that he can use.

While the defense attorney may be a great analytical thinker, he may not have time to listen to the defendant's life story. For that reason, every defendant should invest the time and energy to present that life story.

A life story can make all the difference in the world when it comes to sentencing. Indeed, our team has worked closely with many federal judges. Our website includes two interviews that my partner Michael did with federal judges. Michael asked those judges what steps a person could take to influence the judge's decision. Each judge responded by saying that, when it comes to sentencing, they want to hear from defendants.

Our interviews with both judges are available for free through our Prison Professors YouTube channel, under the following playlist:

» Judge Mark Bennett from the Northern District of Iowa

» Judge Stephen Bough from the Western District of Missouri

  - How to Prepare for Sentencing:
  - https://www.youtube.com/playlist?list=PLf7W0veN3NWbq9nzGNmhQliFbqmaXz26y

If you cannot access the link because you're reading this book in print, simply Google How to Prepare for Sentencing + Prison Professors and you'll find our helpful videos on YouTube or text the following word, to the following number:

» Text word: Sentence

» Text to number: 44222

    o You'll get an automatic brochure sent to your phone.

Defense Attorney's Position:

Some defense attorneys support a pro-active sentence-mitigation plan, while other defense attorneys resist such initiatives. Why?

As stated above, attorneys are great analytical thinkers. Since they know it's the prosecutor's burden to prove a case, they operate out of an abundance of caution. They do not want to introduce any evidence that a prosecutor could use against their client.

Since most defendants start out in denial, incapable of fully appreciating the system or the charges against them, some attorneys do not want their clients to say anything.

Attorneys may have invested considerable amounts of time to construct an elaborate defense. They do not want their clients to make statements that prosecutors may twist, making it more difficult for the attorney to argue for leniency at sentencing. Defense attorneys may prefer to rely upon case law, facts, and what the prosecutor could prove.

We have a different perspective. Our team has interacted with more than 1,000 people that have gone through the criminal justice system. We've had personal interactions with state and federal judges.

Based on our experience, we're convinced that defendants put themselves in a far better position when they engineer an effective sentence-mitigation plan. When a person creates and executes on an effective sentence-mitigation strategy, that individual does immense service to his defense attorney.

In our view, an effective sentence-mitigation plan will strive to achieve several outcomes:

» It will help the judge see and understand the defendant as an individual,

» It will help the judge grasp influences that led the defendant to the current situation,

» It will help the judge see aspects of the defendant's life that could not be conveyed by the defense attorney's eloquence alone,

» It will help the judge see the defendant in his own environment,

» It will help the judge learn what other people in the community think about the defendant.

Engineering an effective sentence-mitigation plan does not excuse the misconduct or litigate the case. In fact, a sentence-mitigation plan does just the opposite. It is a strategy to show the judge why the defendant is worthy of mercy. It would not serve a defendant's interest to minimize culpability, or to blame anyone. If referring to the criminal conduct at all, the sentence-mitigation plan should focus on some key points, including:

1. Show an understanding and an appreciation for the victim's pain, suffering, or loss.

2. Show influences that led the defendant to become involved in the instant offense.
3. Show what the defendant has learned from the experience.
4. Show what steps the defendant has taken to reconcile with society, the victims, and his community to make things right.
5. Articulate a coherent plan to show why the defendant will never break the law again.

What if I Go to Trial?

As stated in previous lessons, the vast majority of people charged in a criminal case start off with a not-guilty plea. Their defense attorneys then assess the evidence and the risks of proceeding through trial, then negotiate the most favorable plea-agreement possible. Still, a small percentage of defendants maintain their innocence and proceed through trial.

If a defendant proceeds through trial, and is found guilty, that defendant may want to appeal. In that case, the defendant will want to create a sentence-mitigation plan that does not in any way threaten the prospects for an appeal. Accordingly, he should refrain from discussing any aspects of the case. Instead, such a strategy should focus exclusively on helping the judge get to know him as a person.

There is always an opportunity to create a mitigation strategy. It is equivalent to building a sales presentation. And how do we accomplish that goal? We begin by thinking about our audience. A sentence-mitigation strategy has an audience of one: the judge.

» What steps can you take to differentiate yourself from every other defendant that comes before the judge?

First Person Approach:

Let your lawyer argue the law and deal with the evidence against you. When it comes to articulating the story of your life, use your own words, in a first-person voice. From our perspective, this is a common sense.

Your lawyer is a professional advocate, skilled in the arts of persuasion. Even if the most notorious criminal retained your attorney, a professional code of ethics would require your attorney to provide the most zealous defense possible. After decades of practicing law, judges know that the defense attorney is going to argue for leniency at sentencing.

While deliberating over the appropriate sentence, the judge isn't too concerned with arguments on case law. He has read the case law; he has his own opinion. On the other hand, he doesn't know much about the defendant.

Prior to sentencing, defendants have an opportunity to influence the outcome. Again, a defendant does well when he starts from the premise that he's about to make the biggest sale of his life. The only question is how well he has prepared, or how much time, energy, and resources he wants to invest to build a persuasive case.

Multi-Tiered Plan:

Our team believes that an effective sentence-mitigation plan should begin at the soonest possible time. No one can change the past, but any of us can begin crafting a story that will show who we are as individuals and how we got here. We're big believers in a multi-tiered strategy that includes:

» A personal sentencing narrative

» A strategic character-reference letter campaign

» A sentencing video

» A sentence-mitigation story of community service

Sentencing Narratives:

Based on what we've learned from judges, we believe that defendants serve themselves well when they write first-person, sentencing narratives. For defendants that have pled guilty, the sentencing narratives should adhere to the five-point list stated above, but that we'll repeat again here:

1. Show an understanding and an appreciation for the victim's pain, suffering, or loss.
2. Show influences that led the defendant to become involved in the instant offense.
3. Show what the defendant has learned from the experience.
4. Show what steps the defendant has taken to reconcile with society, the victims, and his community to make things right.
5. Articulate a coherent plan to show why the defendant will never break the law again.

If a jury or judge convicted the defendant after a trial, then it's important to consider the appellate strategy.

Either way, a well-constructed narrative should focus on the judge's perceptions, using the five-point above as a guideline. We've worked with many individuals that prepared effective sentence-mitigation strategies, even though they did not accept responsibility prior to being convicted after a trial.

Every case is different. There is no cookie-cutter approach. And there is no guarantee that a personal sentencing narrative will influence the judge. That said, based on our extensive experience, we're convinced that a defendant that engineers a well-crafted sentence-mitigation strategy will be in a better position than if he were to remain silent, leaving the judge without any clarity on his mindset or the influences that led him into the predicament at hand.

As with any well-structured letter, it's important to begin with thoughts of the audience. Judges get inundated with paperwork. When crafting the letter, think about length. Our recommendation is to write a document of between 1,500 and 3,000 words. Some documents may go longer. Yet in our experience, we've found this word count to be sufficient to write a coherent narrative. Keep in mind that we're advocating for a multi-pronged approach that would include far more than the sentencing narrative.

Defendants should strive to write a highly personal story, adhering to the five-point plan above. The art of writing is re-writing. Take time to get it right. Ask others to read through the document. Other readers may offer guidance that can prove beneficial.

When it's complete, share the letter with your defense attorney and consider his advice on steps to strengthen the document.

Character-Reference Letters:

The second component of an effective sentence-mitigation strategy includes a well-coordinated character-reference letter campaign.

See our Prison Professors YouTube playlist:

» How to Prepare for Sentencing:

» https://www.youtube.com/playlist?list=PLf-7W0veN3NWbq9nzGNmhQliFbqmaXz26y

We reveal what we've learned from judges about character-reference letters. The judges with whom we've spoken tell us that rather than receiving character-reference letters from high powered professionals or celebrities, they want to read letters from people that knew the defendant best. They want to read stories that offer details showing something about the defendant's character.

For example:

» If the defendant volunteered as an athletic coach, perhaps someone from the team could write about memorable experiences of working with the coach.

» If the defendant volunteered in the community, perhaps a program director could write about how the defendant helped someone without expectations of receiving anything in return.

» If the defendant helped a sick neighbor with lawn care, or grocery shopping, that testimonial would show a great deal about the defendant's character.

Ideally, the person that writes the character-reference letter should reveal that the defendant has been open and honest about the criminal behavior. Judges want to know that the defendant has not been deceptive. If the writer feels that the defendant has expressed remorse, then the writer should express what he has seen.

Judges with whom we've spoken told us that ideally, a defendant would be selective. Rather than submitting an overwhelming number of letters, the judges with whom we've spoken said that it's far better to submit a few, well-crafted letters. Based on what we've heard, judges do not want to receive more than a dozen character reference letters—especially if they all present the same message.

Caveats:

Character-reference letters should never make excuses for the defendant. It would not serve the defendant's interest if the character-reference letter:

» Wrote that the defendant wasn't at fault,

» Stated that the government or jury got it wrong,

» Opinionated that the defendant should not be going to prison,

» Followed a template that many others wrote.

Judges want to hear about the defendant's character. That is all. They do not want to hear the writer's opinion about the case, or the fairness of the judicial system. Nor do they want others telling the judge what sentence would be appropriate. Basically, the judge wants to hear from those that know the defendant best. If they know about the defendant's conviction, and they still express a willingness to support him, that says a great deal.

Sentencing-Mitigation Videos:

As with the character-reference letter and the sentencing narrative, the sentence-mitigation video should help the judge get a more full and complete idea of the defendant. We're striving to help the judge know and understand the defendant.

A video can help the defendant bring aspects of his life into the courtroom that the judge may never know. It's said that a picture speaks a thousand words. A well-crafted video can be like 1,000 pictures that tell a moving story about the defendant's life.

The challenge with video production is that it can be very costly to produce. Depending upon preparations and travel costs, artists charge between $5,000 and $25,000 to produce a sentence-mitigation video. Production costs run high because of the specialized equipment and training it takes to script, film, edit, and produce video content.

On the other hand, a defendant that is skilled with a cellphone camera and editing software may accomplish the same objective, at no cost. The goal is to bring into the courtroom what would otherwise be missing.

Ideally, the video should not be any longer than 15 minutes. And during those 15 minutes, every second should count. It should feature b-roll footage that shows the defendant in his own environment. It must tell a story, showing the complexity of the defendant's life and how he interacts with his community. The more people and images in the video, the more effective it becomes.

The most effective video we played a role in producing included more than 30 people. We profiled the client in various locations, including his home, at his places of business, with his clients, and with his employees.

The video featured interviews with family members, employees, and with clients. It spliced in video-footage showing the results of his work and his contributions to the community. In 15 minutes, the video provided the judge with a comprehensive view of the defendant's character, and it made a huge difference. Indeed, the judge commented on what he learned by watching the video. Then he imposed below-guidelines sentence.

Sentence-Mitigation Story:

Finally, defendants that have the time and energy may want to build a comprehensive story of mitigation. This strategy can include participation in a course, or the creation of a course. It can include a biography, or some type of vehicle that shows the defendant's commitment to making things right. Visit our website at ResilientCourses.com for more insight into our Straight-A Guide sentence-mitigation programs.

Conclusion:

Our team feels strongly that when a defendant invests the time, resources, and energy to architect and build these multi-part sentence-mitigation strategies, they advance prospects for the best, possible outcome. Since each component takes a long time to prepare, we urge defendants to begin at the soonest possible time. Ideally, the sentence-mitigation strategy should be well developed before the pre-sentence investigation takes place. We'll discuss the pre-sentence investigation in the next chapter.

Chapter 7

What Should I Know About the Pre-sentence Investigation Report?

After a person pleads guilty or is found guilty, the presentence investigation will be the next step. For more details, check out Rule 32 of the *U.S. Rules of Criminal Procedure* in the federal system. Each state system has a similar rule in the book of criminal procedure.

In federal cases, probation officers conduct these investigations to help sentencing judges and others evaluate the background of the person. The investigation culminates with an all-important presentence investigation report (PSI or PSR—used interchangeably). The report will include recommendations, based on guidelines and the probation officer's opinion. Sentencing judges will consider recommendations from the PSR when imposing sentence.

Besides the importance of the PSR for sentencing, people should pay close attention to the process because the report also will play a significant role in the person's life if he is sentenced to prison. Information in the PSR influences how authorities classify the prisoner, when he will be released, and what level of liberty he will have after he gets out of prison.

To preserve rights and to self-advocate once inside, it's crucial to understand everything about the presentence investigation before it begins. Best-practice preparations require a person to invest the time and energy to understand the process well *before* the sentencing hearing, or even the investigation begins.

If a defense attorney fails to stress the importance of the PSR, be wary. In prison, the PSR will be the main document administrators will use to make assessments, especially at the start of the journey.

- » Case managers will use the document to consider the severity of the offense;
- » Counselors will use the document to determine who can visit the offender;
- » Educational administrators will use the PSR to determine whether the prisoner is *required* to participate in programs;
- » Psychologists will turn to the PSR to see whether the individual is eligible for beneficial programs; and
- » Medical personnel will turn to the PSR to determine whether the prisoner merits medical attention

Once the court accepts the PSR, it will follow the person until his journey concludes. If there are errors in the PSR, and the probation officer refuses to make adjustments, then it's absolutely critical to ask the judge to address these errors in the Statement of Reasons, which we'll describe below.

Beginning the Investigation:

The probation officer assigned to the case will begin the investigation by becoming familiar with the government's version of the offense. Then, the probation officer will schedule a face-to-face. The meeting may take place at the person's home, in the probation office, over the phone, or in the facility holding the person if he's in custody. Prior to the meeting, the probation officer will have insight on the case from the prosecutor and the investigators. The purpose of the meeting is to collect information from the person being investigated, if he's willing to offer it.

The probation officer will ask the person what he has to say about the offense. He'll also ask about the offender's personal background. Among other things, the probation officer will ask about:

» Family history,

» Education,

» Criminal background,

» Employment history,

» Substance-abuse background,

» Medical condition, and

» Financial status.

Anyone going through a PSR investigation should remember probation officers are law-enforcement officers. If the probation officer believes the person lied, or provided misleading information, or if he believes the offender tried to influence others inappropriately, the probation officer may make things worse.

The probation officer could charge the offender with obstruction of justice if he believed the offender tried to interfere with, manipulate, or subvert his investigation. With such a recommendation, the judge may add additional time to a defendant's sentence.

Probation officers have huge caseloads and it may feel as if they're cynical. The investigator will interview the offender's family members, check the offender's school records, and obtain official records of the offender's previous legal problems.

The probation officer also will speak with previous employers, check with creditors, and search for information to verify the offender's statements about his medical condition.

A person may reserve his right to remain silent during the investigation. But if he chooses to communicate, he should understand that any lies or attempts to mislead the probation officer could result in a longer or more severe sentence. We recommend honesty and good preparation before the PSR interview.

Some people refuse to provide any information to the probation officer. They may have valid reasons for wanting to remain silent.

But if the person doesn't participate in the PSR investigation, the probation officer's writing will only reflect the government's version of events.

Appellate strategy may influence a person's strategy. He may choose not to answer questions about the offense. If that is the case, the offender should be courteous, explaining that for appellate reasons, he cannot discuss the case. He may want to cooperate with the investigation in ways that will not jeopardize his rights.

We recommend that unless the offender has good reason, he ought to cooperate with the investigation. In fact, we urge defendants to prepare the sentence-mitigation strategy long before the PSR interview, and to provide as much documentation as possible to the probation officer.

By giving the officer the personal narrative, the person makes the probation officer's job easier.

Probation officers sometimes cut and paste entire paragraphs or pages from the narrative into the report.

This strategy allows the person to influence a document that will prove enormously influential while the person serves his sentence.

The PSR will influence administrators that the prisoner may never meet. For example, when making the initial classification of where a person serves the sentence, administrators will rely upon the PSR. Others will use the PSR to determine who can visit. On top of all that, the PSR will include information that determines whether the person gets a lower-bunk pass, qualifies to participate in beneficial programs, and for other crucial issues that can influence release dates.

Once inside prison, a *Unit Team* will meet with the prisoner. Administrators on the team—case managers and counselors—will consider the PSR and the record a person accumulates during his confinement.

For those reasons, prior to going inside, people should invest time to understand the myriad ways a PSR will influence the prison term. Then he can make a more competent decision on whether to provide more, rather than less information.

Those who've pled guilty should understand that the probation officer has the authority to recommend a significant downward adjustment from the sentencing guidelines. If the person convinces the officer that he provided a full and candid description of his criminal actions and demonstrates genuine remorse for his criminal behavior, the officer may recommend that the person gets credit for "acceptance of responsibility."

The probation officer's recommendation in the PSR isn't binding on the judge, but it is influential. In our experience, people that express remorse for their actions help themselves. If they can persuade the court that their criminal behavior was an aberration rather than a pattern of behavior or a *criminal lifestyle,* they usually receive lower sentences than those who refuse to cooperate with the presentence investigation. Likewise, those who choose to exercise their rights to silence may be portrayed as unremorseful. Judges would likely take a lack of remorse into consideration at sentencing.

The PSR Report Itself:

Once the officer finishes the investigation, court rules require him to write his complete report "in a non-argumentative style." After describing the details of the offense and other identifying data, a model PSR from the Southern District of New York contains headings as follows.

Offense Conduct:

In this section, the probation officer writes the government's version of events and may describe discrepancies that the offender wanted inserted in the document.

Victim Impact Statement:

If the crime had an identifiable victim, the probation officer may give the victim an opportunity to describe how the offense impacted him (or her).

Defendants' Participation:

If the offender was convicted along with others in the offense, the probation officer may detail the conduct of each defendant in the case under this heading. This can be prejudicial, because some participants may be much more culpable than others.

Offenders ought to ask the attorney to challenge any information that suggests or insinuates that he participated in the same behavior of others if he did not. Prison staff members who evaluate an offender may not make any distinction between participants. If the PSR indicates that one member of the offense was violent and predatory in nature, that information may have a material influence on all members of the offense as far as prison classifications are concerned.

Obstruction of Justice Adjustment:

If the person obstructed justice in any way, the probation officer may recommend a sentencing enhancement. Examples of obstruction of justice include when an offender tries to influence what others will say during a government investigation.

If the offender calls an individual and says, "Don't talk, or else...." the officer may charge the individual with obstruction of justice and with threatening violence. If so, prison administrators may characterize the offender as being violent in nature, which will prohibit participation in certain beneficial programs.

Acceptance of Responsibility Adjustment:

If the offender is candid about his responsibility, the probation officer may recommend a downward departure from sentencing guidelines. The level of the downward departure will depend upon *when* the offender accepted responsibility.

People that plead guilty early in the criminal justice procedure receive the largest downward departures for acceptance of responsibility. It's a reward for saving the government the time and expense of preparing for trial.

Those who proceeded through trial will have a higher burden to meet in order to receive this benefit. But going to trial does not *necessarily* preclude a person from receiving this sentencing adjustment.

Remember, the judge has discretion, and it's important to build an influential case on why you're worthy of mercy. Acceptance of responsibility can weigh heavily on the judge's decision to grant mercy.

Offense Level Computation:

Criminal statutes and guidelines influence this objective score. Offenders may read about these scores by studying the *U.S. Sentencing Guidelines Manual* which is available in all federal prison law libraries. Those who do not have access to prison law libraries may review online or order the book from a bookstore. Guideline manuals may be too complicated to read for those that do not have a legal background. Our courses at ResilientCourses.com offer some video tutorials.

Criminal History:

This information comes from past criminal convictions. Points are assigned to those who have been convicted for other offenses, and each prior conviction counts against the score. Chapter Four of the *U.S. Sentencing Guidelines Manual* explains how probation officers count the points.

Offender Characteristics:

Probation officers use this section to describe what he learned about the offender through his presentence investigation. It's a subjective description. The offender's family responsibilities also will be discussed as well as the offender's community ties.

If the offender engineered a sentence-mitigation strategy earlier, he may want to share his personal narrative during the PSR interview. Probation officers may cut and paste parts of the narrative into this section. That strategy can prove extremely useful to the person as he goes through the system, both in sentencing and while in prison.

Substance Abuse:

This section describes whether the person suffered from any substance abuse problems in the past. It is an extremely important section. In the federal prison, the BOP has authority to reduce a person's by as much as 12 months if the offender completes a 500-hour drug treatment program during his incarceration.

To qualify for this year off, the BOP will require the offender to provide documentation that he suffered from substance-abuse prior to imprisonment, ideally, during the 12 months that preceded arrest.

The substance-abuse section of the PSR report is an excellent place to document a history of drug abuse or alcoholism that would benefit from treatment. During the PSR investigation, defendants that suffered from alcoholism or abused other drugs should report those experiences.

If those reports meet certain criteria, the defendant may qualify for participation in a drug-treatment program. If he completes the program successfully, he may get out of prison earlier.

People that do not understand the PSR sometimes conceal their history of substance abuse. They mistakenly believe substance abuse of any kind will reflect badly on them at sentencing. Hiding a history of substance abuse may limit access to beneficial programs that could result in a sentence reduction.

Physical Condition:

Here the probation officer describes health problems or medical conditions. If the person suffers from a bad back, has weak knees, or any ailments that may have an impact on his ability to climb onto a top bunk or perform certain duties, he should detail those ailments. If the probation officer documents health conditions in the PSR, it may influence housing assignments.

If possible, it's helpful to get a letter from a physician and medical records. Good preparation includes documentation to support a medical condition. That documentation can help a prisoner self-advocate once his term of imprisonment begins.

For example, a doctor's letter verifying a bad back or weak knees will help an offender secure a coveted lower-bunk pass. That pass can be a blessing for an individual who lacks the strength to climb onto a top bunk.

Education and VT Skills:

The probation officer will ask about education and credentials. To avoid complications, help the probation officer get the information necessary to confirm diplomas and degrees. Administrators in prison will require those that do not have a verified high school education to attend prison-sponsored GED courses for at least 240 hours. They will receive lower wages from their prison work details. Participation in GED classes may have an impact on an ability to earn good time or earned time.

Prison administrators frown upon prisoners who have extensive computer experience. If the PSR indicates that an individual has computer programming skills, administrators may deny that individual access to coveted clerical jobs by placing *computer ban* on his file. Administrative rules may deny camp placement for defendants that have crimes related to sophisticated computer programming and wireless networks.

Employment Record:

Probation officers will check with prior employers to obtain an evaluation of the person's work habits. A good work history may influence the sentencing judge. Also, an extensive work history may help a person advocate for himself if he is seeking a specific job in the prison.

Financial Condition:

Consider all financial liabilities and responsibilities when meeting with the probation officer who is preparing the report. Most criminal convictions result in monetary fines or restitution orders. All felony criminal convictions result in criminal-assessment fees. For some defendants, sentencing courts impose cost-of-confinement fees.

Sentencing judges may choose not to impose fines and cost-of-confinement fees if the person is incapable of paying. Judges are less forgiving when it comes to restitution. Laws may require judges to impose felony-assessment fees.

If the court imposes a monetary penalty, BOP staff members will demand monthly payments. They will consider any funds that pass through the offender's commissary account as being available for such payments. These charges can make life more difficult inside.

If a monetary sanction becomes part of a person's sentence, the offender's attorney ought to ask the judge to specify that the fine is not to be collected until *after* the offender's release from confinement.

If the judge's commitment order specifies that the offender doesn't have to pay the monetary portion of the sanction until the person is released, the BOP will not be able to pressure the person for payments during confinement.

Sentencing Options:

The probation officer discusses options the judge may consider when imposing sentencing. The options are rather limited in that they only offer a monetary fine, probation, or incarceration in some form—either house arrest, a community confinement center, or imprisonment.

Many crimes, particularly offenses related to the distribution of drugs, require mandatory-minimum sentences that preclude sanctions less than imprisonment. One can develop a better understanding of federal sentencing options by reading the most current edition of the very detailed *Federal Sentencing Law And Practice* by Thomas W. Hutchison, et al, and published by West Group.

Factors that May Warrant Departure:

In the federal system, judges must *consider* sentencing guidelines. The guidelines are not mandatory, but most judges use them as a starting point. If the judge chooses to depart from established guidelines for a specific offender, the judge must articulate his reasons during the sentencing hearing.

The probation officer will describe factors that may warrant either a downward or upward departure from the sentencing guidelines. The most common downward departure is when an offender cooperates with the government in the investigation and provides assistance in the prosecution of others. People that place the highest value on getting out of prison at the soonest possible time may choose to cooperate with prosecutors. Such decisions may influence where a person serves his time, and whether that person is ostracized by others in prison.

In rare instances, probation officers may recommend downward departures for other reasons. They may find that a person's situation is markedly different from others that were convicted of the same type of offense. It is a high burden, but in rare cases, people receive downward departures for issues other than cooperating in the prosecution of others.

Upward departures are more common. Judges issue sentences that are harsher than the guidelines when they're convinced that the sentencing guidelines do not reflect the seriousness of the offender's conduct.

The Completed PSR Report:

Following the completion of the PSR, the probation officer will deliver copies of the report to the prosecutor and the offender's attorney. Both parties will have time to review the document. If inaccuracies appear, each party will have an opportunity to object to the perceived errors. Once the objections are noted, the probation officer will determine whether the objections are valid. If so, changes to the PSR will follow.

If the probation officer refuses to make changes that either party wants, that party can bring the matter up with the sentencing judge. The judge will listen to both sides and each side may present evidence to bolster its position. After hearing the arguments, the judge will make a determination. Sometimes, though, the judge may sentence the offender according to his findings at the hearing, but not order changes to the written PSR.

Defense attorneys should be vigilant in efforts to get a PSR that accurately reflects the judge's findings. The BOP will use the PSR for classifications and to make other decisions, which can have a huge influence on how and where the person serves the sentence.

If the judge chooses not to order the probation officer to correct a PSR, the defense attorney may ask the judge to make specific findings in the commitment order, and also in a Statement of Reasons for the sentence.

Statement of Reasons:

In addition to the PSR, the court will submit a Statement of Reasons to the Bureau of Prisons. See Title 28 United States Code Section 994(w)(1)(B), which tells us:

> the written Statement of Reasons for the sentence imposed (which shall include the reason for any departure from the otherwise applicable guideline range and which shall be stated on the written statement of reasons form issued by the Judicial Conference and approved by the United States Sentencing Commission);

In February 2016, the Judicial Conference issued, and the Sentencing Commission approved, Form AE 245B. Section IB4 of the revised form tell us that:

> "comments or factual findings concerning any information in the presentence report, including information that the Federal Bureau of Prisons may rely on when it makes inmate classification, designation, or programming decisions."

The United States Sentencing Commission published a video at the following location that offers more insight into the Statement of Reasons:

» https://www.ussc.gov/education/videos/sentencing-and-guidelines-revised-statement-reasons-form

The Bureau of Prisons will review both the Statement of Reasons and the PSR when classifying a person. For that reason, attorneys should make a strong case to persuade the judge to put specific language in the Statement of Reasons that may help a person qualify for specific BOP programs.

A judge's Statement of Reasons could potentially influence an earlier release date for a person by qualifying him for specific programs that could lead to an earlier transition to home confinement. Program Statement 5322.13 requires the BOP to consider the Statement of Reasons when calculating each prisoner's security level. For that reason, some may argue that the Statement of Reasons may be an excellent remedy to overcome problems with an inaccurate PSR.

Chapter 8

What Examples Can You Provide About Problematic PSRs?

In the previous chapter we discussed the structure of PSR reports and how a Statement of Reasons can help some people overcome problematic PSRs. Probation officers prepare the PSR specifically for the sentencing judge. But the PSR follows the person all the way through the journey.

In fact, our team would argue that the PSR has a bigger influence after the sentence is imposed. After all, a judge likely knows a great deal about the case.

If a defendant engineered an effective sentence-mitigation strategy, as we described in chapter six of this program, the judge will also know a great deal about the person and the influences that led him into the problem. Further, an attorney will likely be there to advocate on the person's behalf.

After the judge imposes the sentence, on the other hand, the defendant will not have an attorney. He will need to advocate on his own behalf. And the PSR will be an essential tool. If the person worked intelligently by engineering an effective sentence-mitigation strategy, he may succeed in getting a more favorable journey through prison. On the other hand, if the PSR is inaccurate, the person may have a harder time overcoming hurdles in prison—when a defense attorney will not be available to help.

For these reasons, we encourage people to review the PSR carefully. Again, this is a critical responsibility. Some factors the offender must especially be concerned about include whether the PSR inaccurately reflects that the offender was a "leader" in the criminal offense.

Any reference to the word "leader" or "organizer" may result in the offender being treated more severely by prison administrators.

If the PSR suggests or identifies the offender as being a leader, and the offender believes such an accusation to be inappropriate, then it is in his best interest to address this problem. Impress upon the attorney to work to correct the inaccuracy in the PSR.

Rather than ordering the probation officer to amend the PSR, the judge may correct the inaccuracy on the Statement of Reasons. Prison officials cannot ignore the Statement of Reasons. And a person in prison may be able to rely upon the statement to clear matters up through administrative remedy—which we describe in a later chapter.

Drug Offenders:

Drug offenders should review the quantity of drugs the PSR attributes to them. Frequently, people played relatively minor roles in drug distribution networks, but the PSR may insinuate greater responsibility.

If it suggests that the offender was responsible for all the drugs involved in a large conspiracy, prison officials may take the conservative approach and classify him more harshly.

If the PSR suggests a person is responsible for large quantities of drugs, he may be sent to a higher-security prison. He may be ineligible for camp placement.

When it comes time for halfway house or home confinement, administrators may deny him.

For these reasons, people should do their best to get a PSR that accurately reflects culpability. And if the probation officer will not make the adjustment, the prisoner should work with counsel to get specific language in the Statement of Reasons at sentencing.

Violence in PSR:

Besides leadership roles and high drug quantities, we've seen other significant problems with inaccurate PSR reports. For example, if the PSR alludes to violence, use of weapons, or ties to organized crime, prison officials will classify the person more harshly.

We've heard of attorneys that mislead their clients. They diminish the relevance of the PSR, saying the judge already knows what he is going to do. Such advice may reflect the attorney's eagerness to conclude his representation in the case and move on to new matters.

A judge may have an idea of the sentence that he is going to impose, but the PSR has more lasting ramifications on a person going to prison.

An inaccurate PSR report may result in a prisoner serving his sentence in a harsher environment and it may deprive him of access to special programs. Some offenders serve more time in prison than necessary because of inaccurate PSR reports. Once the report is submitted to the BOP, making an amendment to it is—for all practical purposes—unlikely.

Influence the Process:

The best time to influence possibilities for an accurate PSR is before the investigation takes place. In chapter six, we discussed the importance of engineering a sentence-mitigation plan. A best-case scenario would be to present the probation officer with a well-thought-out sentencing narrative (that counsel has approved) during the investigation.

When the probation officer asks the offender what he has to say about his role in the office, the offender may respond:

> "I knew that I was going to be nervous when I got here. For that reason, I've taken the time to write out a document. Please review this document and incorporate as much as possible into your report. I'll be submitting it, through counsel, to my judge at sentencing."

We've seen probation officers cut-and-paste entire portions of the defendant's statement into the PSR. Provide the probation officer with a written copy, and perhaps a digital version as well. Make it as easy as possible. By influencing the PSR, the person advances possibilities to advocate for himself while he is inside the BOP.

On the other hand, if the person receives an inaccurate report, ask counsel to work earnestly to correct inaccuracies as early as possible. If the probation officer refuses to amend the PSR, then the next best time to object is at sentencing.

The offender should request the sentencing judge to order the necessary corrections. If that opportunity passes, the offender may be stuck with the inaccuracies for the duration of his sentence.

As discussed previously, all is not lost, so long as the judge agrees to clarify judicial findings in the Statement of Reasons. The BOP will consider those judicial remarks if they differ from the PSR.

Offenders who do not take the time to understand the significance of the PSR frequently encounter problems that could have been avoided. Even if errors were made in the initial draft, the offender must not underestimate the importance of having all errors corrected and ensuring that the court orders the erroneous report destroyed.

People that have more financial resources might consider hiring a post-conviction or sentencing specialist. Get advice on all issues regarding PSR reports. Sometimes, it makes sense to hire a retired probation officer, or sentencing expert, to draft a mock report.

The defense attorneys may submit the report, along with the expert's credentials, for the judge to consider. A person should make every possible effort to ensure that he is portrayed accurately and in a favorable way, not only for the sentencing judge, but also for prison authorities.

For example, consider stories from people with whom our team has worked.

***Raymond*:**

Raymond, an offender who was convicted of conspiracy to distribute cocaine, played a minor role in his offense. He allowed others to use his telephone to facilitate their drug transactions. Raymond was not privy to the quantity of drugs being sold, nor to the number of transactions that took place over his telephone line. Yet the PSR report indicated over 20 kilograms of cocaine were sold and that all conspirators, including, Raymond, were equally culpable.

The sentencing judge had listened to all the testimony at trial. He knew that Raymond was a minor player in the conspiracy. He found Raymond less culpable than the others and gave him a downward departure from the sentencing guidelines because of his minor role.

The judge did not, however, order an amendment of the PSR. As a result, case managers in the BOP used the PSR to classify him. As a result of the inaccuracy, they deemed him a "serious offender," meaning he could not get camp placement. Raymond tried to get the judge to amend the PSR several times while he served the term. But the judge ruled the matter moot because Raymond received the downward departure at sentencing, and he refused to make any further adjustments.

Neither Raymond nor his attorney appreciated the significance of his PSR prior to sentencing. At sentencing, the attorney persuaded the judge that the PSR inaccurately portrayed Raymond as an equal participant in the conspiracy. Yet he didn't attempt to change the PSR itself. Accordingly, Raymond was sentenced appropriately, but he served his term in more severe conditions than other similarly situated offenders because his PSR was inaccurate.

Raymond showed his case manager the sentencing transcripts. The judge clearly ruled that Raymond was less culpable than the others and sentenced him accordingly. The case manager, however, said the PSR governed all classification decisions.

Again, this is a situation where the judge could have clarified Raymond's culpability in the Statement of Reasons. Since he did not have that clarity, he served a harsher sentence.

Carlos:

Carlos owned a small chain of retail stores in New Jersey. He was convicted of tax evasion and sentenced to serve four years in prison. When interviewed during the presentence investigation, the probation officer asked Carlos whether he had any problems with substance abuse. Thinking that admitting to any form of substance abuse would result in an unfavorable impression, Carlos told the probation officer that he did not abuse drugs.

In fact, Carlos smoked marijuana occasionally for fifteen years. He drank alcohol regularly, sometimes until he blacked out. Had he admitted this substance abuse to the probation officer, his PSR would have reflected Carlos' experience with controlled substances, including alcohol. Instead, the PSR stated what Carlos indicated during the investigation: no history of substance abuse.

When Carlos began serving his sentence, he learned about the drug treatment programs. He also learned that nonviolent offenders who completed the 500-hour program successfully could get out of prison earlier. Carlos wanted to apply for the program. He approached the psychologist who administered the drug treatment program for an interview.

When the psychologist read Carlos' PSR, she noted no indication of substance abuse. She told Carlos that he would not be eligible for any time off his sentence because there wasn't any prior history of substance abuse. Carlos explained that he had used marijuana for 15 years. He didn't admit his drug use to the probation officer, he said, because he didn't want to make a bad impression.

The psychologist expressed sympathy. Yet without documentation of prior substance abuse, he didn't qualify for the program. She told him that she needed some type of documentation before she could admit him. As a result of his not preparing in advance of his meeting with the probation officer, Carlos had a harder time.

Randall:

Randall is a 64-year old medical doctor. For the past 30 years he operated a cardiology practice. Randall was sentenced to serve 36-months for violating the laws pertaining to health care. Randall's PSR confirmed that he held an undergraduate degree from Columbia University and a medical degree from Cornell. It did not verify that he graduated from high school.

During his first week in prison, administrators ordered Randall to the education department. The teacher told Randall that he had to participate in a GED class. Randall said such a request was silly, as he has practiced as a physician for over 30 years.

The BOP staff member said, "That doesn't mean anything. A lot of people have advanced degrees but don't have a GED. We require all our prisoners who lack a high school diploma to participate in the GED program."

Randall thought the order absurd and told the teacher that he would show her his PSR, which verified his educational credentials. The teacher said she was not interested in reading about those credentials.

Since the report did not indicate that Randall had a GED, the teacher was requiring him to participate in the class. Randall refused and was promptly taken to segregation for refusing an order. He also was sanctioned with loss of commissary.

***Rich*:**

Rich pled guilty to an indictment charging several defendants with organized crime involving extortion and murder. Rich's role, however, was minor and he was sentenced to serve approximately five years as a result of his conviction.

He was a mortgage broker, and he pled guilty to completing fraudulent loan applications. Other codefendants that were charged on the same indictment as Rich received sentences of life imprisonment.

Rich's probation officer conducted the PSR for all defendants on the indictment. When Rich appeared for his interview, he was accompanied by his defense counsel. The defense counsel heard everything said during Rich's interview, and Rich was cooperative throughout the proceeding.

When Rich and his attorney reviewed the PSR, however, it was clear that the probation officer had confused some of Rich's codefendant's defiant statements and inappropriately applied them to Rich. The PSR insinuated, inaccurately, that Rich was involved in the entire criminal conspiracy.

At the sentencing hearing, Rich's attorney succeeded in showing the clear error in the PSR. The judge ordered the PSR to be amended, and the probation officer made the changes. The judge sentenced Rich appropriately.

When Rich reported to prison, however, he learned that his case manager used the original, erroneously prepared PSR. Consequently, the case manager told Rich that he would never be eligible for camp placement and that he may not be eligible for halfway house placement, either.

Rich contacted his attorney and the lawyer filed a motion requesting the judge to issue an order for the BOP to use the correct report. The court refused to grant the order, stating that such issues should have been resolved at the sentencing hearing. As a result of the error, Rich continues to serve his sentence in harsher conditions.

Final Word:

To avoid the type of problems that make confinement more difficult, do everything possible to get an accurate PSR. Raymond, Carlos, Randall, Rich, and many other federal prisoners struggle through harsher conditions because they didn't fully understand the importance of a PSR.

To get a more complete understanding of the PSR, it may make sense to read Rule 32 of the Federal Rules of Criminal Procedure (or the equivalent rule in a state system) to grasp the intended purpose of the presentence investigation.

Chapter 9

What Happens at the Sentencing Hearing and After?

In most cases, after a person enters a guilty plea, or after a jury finds a person guilty, the judge sets a sentencing date. Those sentencing dates may be extended if the person is cooperating with authorities.

Sometimes a person doesn't get sentenced for several years after the guilty plea. In most cases, a person will face a sentencing hearing within a few months of pleading guilty.

On the other hand, our team has worked with clients that waited 10 years before they had resolution. They committed a crime, faced civil proceedings, waited through criminal proceedings, cooperated with authorities. From the time of the crime, and the time the sentence was imposed, 10 years passed. Every case is different.

To prepare for sentencing, the defense attorney will prepare a memorandum. That memorandum will summarize the defendant's conduct, include points of law, and offer reasons why the defendant deserves leniency. The prosecutor will submit a memorandum. In most cases, the prosecutor will argue for a harsher sentence.

In earlier chapters, we've emphasized the importance of engineering a sentence-mitigation strategy. For reasons described earlier, our team recommends a three- or four-pronged approach that includes:

1. A first-person sentencing narrative,
2. A character-letter writing campaign, and if resources permit,
3. A sentencing video,
4. A comprehensive sentence-mitigation plan.

By investing the time and energy to prepare, the person can help the judge get a better understanding of what happened. In addition to the four-pronged sentence-mitigation strategy, the person should also consider speaking at sentencing. Every defendant has a right to speak during the "allocution" phase, but not every defendant chooses to speak.

Why?

Sometimes, defense attorneys discourage defendants from speaking. By nature, defense attorneys are risk averse. They may have worked very hard preparing elaborate arguments.

An emotional defendant may undermine the defense attorney's arguments by minimizing responsibility. Some defendants can talk themselves into a harsher sentence. A well-prepared defendant, on the other hand, can be his best advocate during allocution.

Judges have told members of our team that they want to know as much as possible about the defendant before sentencing. Too often, defendants squander the opportunity to make a persuasive plea for mercy at sentencing. They may talk about how they're going to miss their family and how they've been going to church. Every defendant will miss his family. Going to church may or may not be relevant to the judge.

Defendant's advance their pursuit of mercy when they convince the judge that they understand the gravity of their crime and the impact the crime has had on society. Judges want to know defendants have introspected, and a well-prepared defendant can make that case during allocution. In earlier chapters, we've addressed our thoughts on how a defendant should prepare for the sentencing hearing. The videos that we include with our course also provide tips to prepare.

What Happens at the Sentencing Hearing?

At the sentencing hearing, the defense attorney, the prosecuting attorney, and possibly the probation officer will take turns arguing their issues regarding the presentence investigation report. Sometimes, the prosecutors will call upon victims of the crime to have their say. And the person being sentenced may call upon character witnesses, too.

At some point, the prosecutor may request a specific sentence. The defense attorney will argue that the sentence should be less than what the prosecutor recommends. If a person chooses to make a statement, it will usually be after the attorneys and other witnesses have had their say.

We're convinced that acceptance of responsibility and an expression of remorse is a better strategy than standing stone-faced before a sentencing judge. Eloquence or flowery prose is not nearly as important as sincerity. People being sentenced should know that judges are not gullible or soft. By being truthful and unpretentious, a person can advance prospects for mercy.

After Sentencing:

Once the judge imposes sentence, defendants may ask the judge to rule on collateral matters. Those being sentenced to federal prison may ask the judge to clarify the record, with statements on matters that include:

1. Payment schedules for monetary penalties associated with the sentence;
2. A recommendation for a particular institution;
3. Those with sentences of less than 10 years may request time to get their affairs in order and report to prison voluntarily;
4. Recommendations for specific programs that could, potentially, influence release dates, if appropriate.

Payment Schedules and the Financial Responsibility Plan (FRP):

When judges impose monetary fines or restitution as a part of the sentence, administrators in prison will want to collect. The counselor, case manager, or unit manager will try to enroll the person in a Financial Responsibility Plan (FRP). It's a "voluntary" program, with strings attached.

If the person does not participate in the FRP, administrators will withhold privileges. For example, by not participating, counselors may deny the person access to commissary, the telephone, or visiting.

Participating in the FRP plan requires the person to maintain a balance of funds in the prison commissary account. Payments toward FRP will come out automatically, on a specified date. If the person does not have funds available, sanctions will follow.

Administrators will compute payments in accordance with the amount of money that passes through the commissary account over a six-month period.

To avoid hassles associated with the FRP program, the defendant may make a request during the sentencing hearing. Some judges will agree to suspend any monetary payments until after the person is released from prison. Another option would be to ask the judge to set FRP payments at a fixed amount during sentencing. Otherwise, prison officials may order the person to make burdensome monetary payments that make life more difficult in prison.

Ordinarily, the minimum payment to participate in an FRP program is $25 per quarter. But some people pay more than $1,000 per month toward the FRP. High payments can be a burden on both families and on the person serving time.

Requesting Specific Institutions:

During the sentencing hearing, the person may request to serve his sentence in a specific institution. Later in this chapter we'll describe different security levels.

If a defendant is serving a sentence that will require more than 10 years of imprisonment, or if there are other factors involved, the person will have to serve his sentence in a low-security prison or higher. A person should understand security levels as well as the custody-and-classification system before asking for a specific institution.

To the extent possible, the person should also learn

as much as possible about program availability in specific institutions. As a result of our consulting work, our team has a wide network of contacts with people that are serving sentences in the Bureau of Prisons. We gather information about specific prisons, and programs in specific prisons. Then we make the information available through ResilentCourses.com.

Some judges will agree to recommend a specific institution. In the federal system, judges sentence a defendant "to the custody of the attorney general." That means the person is being transferred from the judicial branch of government to the executive branch of government.

The attorney general oversees the Bureau of Prisons, and the Bureau of Prisons has ultimate discretion on where a person serves the sentence. Although a defendant may request a specific institution, and the judge may recommend a specific institution, the Bureau of Prisons is not bound to follow the judge's recommendation.

For that reason, a person should understand more about the prison-designation process. Then, the person should work closely with counsel. To increase the chances of getting to the best prison, the attorney should think strategically when framing the request.

As an example of a request that went wrong, we offer the story of Andrew. A federal judge sentenced Andrew to serve 15 months in prison. At the sentencing hearing, the attorney requested the judge to recommend that Andrew serve his sentence at the Lompoc Federal Prison Camp. The judge agreed. Yet when Andrew received his letter of designation, he learned that the Federal Bureau of Prisons ordered him to serve his term at a federal detention center.

Andrew had a valid reason for wanting to serve his sentence at the federal prison camp in Lompoc. Yet his attorney failed to ask the sentencing judge to cite those reasons on his Statement of Reasons. As a result, the BOP did not place the appropriate weight to the judge's recommendation.

The more people know about the custody, classification, and designation process, the more effective they may be in getting to the best possible prison, given personal circumstances.

Prison Classifications Levels:

All federal prisons fall into one of five different security levels: minimum, low, medium, high, or administrative.

Administrative-level facilities are designed to hold prisoners from any security level. That means an administrative facility may be holding mass murderers together with people that mailed envelopes with fake postage stamps. Because administrative facilities hold such diverse groups of prisoners, life inside of them is strictly controlled.

Prisoners held in administrative facilities are usually there for a specific purpose besides serving the sentence. Their freedom of movement is strictly controlled.

For the most part, administrative facilities are like large county jails, holding any type of offender. Generally, they serve five purposes:

1. Holding people near the courthouse to ease transportation for judicial proceedings;

2. As transit facilities while prisoners on being transferred to other prisons;
3. As medical centers, where staff and equipment are available to treat complicated health concerns of the BOP prisoner population.
4. As high-security facilities that limit a prisoner's ability to interact with the public or with other prisoners.
5. As witness-protection facilities for offenders that may be particularly vulnerable in general population.

The vast majority of federal prisoners serve their sentences in minimum, low, medium, or high security prisons. Ordinarily, authorities hold people in administrative facilities for limited amounts of time, and for specific reasons. As a result of the Bureau of Prison's complex system of classifying prisoners, the prisoners held in each respective prison will have similar security needs.

Seven factors determine an institution's security level. They include:

1. The use of mobile patrols that drive around the institution's perimeter 24 hours each day;
2. Gun towers located around a prison's outside perimeter from which armed BOP guards monitor the activities inside of a prison;
3. The perimeter barriers that separate the prison from the community;
4. The use of detection devices like metal detectors

and sound guns that can intercept prisoner conversations;

5. The internal security features like locks on individual doors and bars on windows;
6. Specific housing issues, such as whether prisoners are confined in locked rooms, cages, or open dormitories; and finally,
7. The ratio of inmates to staff members.

The higher the security level of an institution, the more stringent the security needs. The most secure federal prison in the United States is the Administrative-maximum security prison at Florence, Colorado (ADX), In the ADX, authorities have strict control over all movement and interactions.

United States penitentiaries (USP's) are high-security institutions. They can have higher rates of violence because they hold prisoners with violent backgrounds in more open settings.

Medium-security prisons (Federal Correctional Institutions—FCI's) also have relatively high-security needs. They generally hold prisoners with up to 30 years remaining to serve. These long-term prisoners may bring higher levels of volatility to an institution.

Low-security FCIs maintain a substantial degree of control, but they are more open than medium-FCIs or high-security USPs.

Federal Prison Camps or Satellite Prison Camps (FPCs and SCPs), on the other hand, hold prisoners that the BOP has determined need the least amount of supervision or security controls. People in camps have about as much exposure to violence as people shopping in a grocery store. Violence can happen, but it's rare and isolated because most of the people in camp do not want disciplinary infractions that can lead them to higher security prisons.

Custody and Security Scoring:

After a federal judge imposes a sentence of incarceration, the U.S. Marshals will send the judgment order and the PSR to the BOP office in Grand Prairie, Texas. State prison systems will have a similar process, with a group of administrators determining where the person will serve the sentence.

Officials that will never meet the person will make a determination on where he should serve the sentence. For that reason, when requesting a judicial recommendation at sentencing, defense attorneys should ask the judge to do more than recommend an institution. Attorneys should provide the judge with specific reasons why one institution is in the best interest of society and the attorney should request the judge to state those reasons in the judgment order.

Ideally, the judge's Statement of Reasons will make specific findings on why the institution is appropriate. For example, there may be a specific program that would benefit the person. Or there may be external reasons why confinement in a specific institution would serve the needs of society. If the judge provides a reason, officials in the BOP will place more weight on the judge's recommendation.

The BOP published a Custody and Classification Manual (Manual) which describes guidelines prison administrators use when designating an individual's place of imprisonment. The Manual is available on the Bureau of Prisons' website at www.BOP (dot) gov under Program Statement 5100.07 (check the latest version).

Interested parties that have access to the Internet should consult the www.BOP.gov website. It includes considerable amounts of useful information, including program statements. Anyone going into the federal prison system would be wise to review Program Statement 5100.07 to understand how prison behavior influences placement in specific facilities.

Although a person may begin with one custody and security score, the scores may change over time. Those changes could result in transfers to other institutions.

In an effort to ensure all designation and transfer decisions are made without favoritism given to an individual's social or economic status, the Manual provides a matrix which allows BOP case managers to arrive at an objective score that will determine each offender's security needs.

Once case managers identify an offender's security level, he will be designated to a corresponding facility. Basically, the manual uses a point system for two types of offender scoring.

» The Base Score, evaluates an offender's legal status;

» The Custody Score, evaluates an offender's prison behavior.

With the Base Score, an offender can score from a minimum of zero points to a maximum of seven points. It assigns points to such issues as:

- » Whether the individual has a detainer filed against him (pending additional legal action);
- » The severity of the current offense;
- » Any type of prior commitment;
- » Any history of escape attempts;
- » Any history of violence; and
- » An individual's pre-commitment status (whether he self-surrendered).

On this Base Score, the lower the number of points, the better for an offender.

With the Custody Score, an offender can score from a minimum of ten points to a maximum of 30 points. It evaluates:

The percentage of time served as related to expected stay in prison;

- » History of drug or alcohol abuse;
- » Mental / psychological stability;
- » The seriousness and quantity of disciplinary infractions received while in custody;
- » Frequency of disciplinary problems during the past year;
- » Level of responsibility demonstrated during incarceration; and
- » Family ties.

On this Custody score, the higher the number of points, the better for the offender.

After BOP administrators calculate a Base Score and a Custody Score, they plug the two separate numbers into a formula which will provide the administrators with a total security-level score.

For male offenders, barring special circumstances outlined in Chapter Seven of the Manual, total score between zero and five points may qualify for camp placement. Scores between six and eight points usually are held in low-security prisons.

If a person scores between nine and fourteen points, he generally will be designated to serve his sentence in a medium-security prison.

If the score is higher than fifteen points on the security-level scoring system, the person may go to a high-security federal penitentiary.

For female offenders, the BOP uses a similar system, but assigns different points to the criteria determining each female offender's security level. Females with zero to ten points usually are designated to minimum-security facilities; females with eleven to twenty-one points usually are designated to low-security facilities; and females who score higher than twenty-two points usually are designated to a high-security facility for women.

Management Variables and Public Safety Factors:

Despite an offender's classification scoring, some additional circumstances may play a role in an offender's security level. The Bureau of Prisons accommodates these factors through the use of Management Variables and Public Safety Factors.

Management Variables identify criteria that may have an impact on where an individual serves his sentence. Case Managers can apply a Management Variable to an individual offender for the following reasons:

1. Judicial Recommendation: when the offender's sentencing judge recommended a specific institution;
2. Release Residence/Planning: to help an offender remain close to his area of release;
3. Population Management: to maintain balance in a facility's inmate population;
4. Central Inmate Monitoring: to monitor specifically targeted offenders;
5. Medical / Psychiatric Treatment: to provide medical attention;
6. Program Participation: to allow inmates to participate in programs available at only certain facilities;
7. Work Cadre: to make use of inmate labor;
8. Mariel Cuban; to monitor a group of prisoners whom the BOP identifies as having caused widespread disruption in the federal prison system;
9. Greater Security: to confine prisoners in higher-security facilities than for which they would otherwise qualify; and,
10. Lesser Security: to confine prisoners in lower-security facilities than for which they would otherwise qualify.

The Bureau of Prisons applies Public Safety Factors to screen offenders that administrators deem may require a more secure prison than the classification point system indicates. Public Safety Factors are applied for the following reasons:

1. Disruptive Group: for inmates who are identified as belonging to a group suspected of subverting prison management policies;
2. Greatest Severity Offense: to screen leaders of criminal enterprises, racketeers, and offenders convicted of serious crimes;
3. Sex Offenders: to monitor inmates who have been convicted of sexual crimes, including Internet pornography;
4. Threat to Government Official: to monitor inmates who have been identified as seriously threatening government officials;
5. Deportable Alien: to keep track of prisoners who may be deported at the conclusion of their sentences;
6. Sentence Length: to track offenders with long sentences;
7. Serious Escape: to monitor prisoners who have escaped from secure prisons; and,
8. Prison Disturbance: to monitor prisoners identified as having participated in prior riots, strikes, or other subversive behavior.

After BOP administrators consider all factors, including the Classification score, Management Variables, and Public Safety Factors, they will designate the person to a particular prison. The stated objective of the BOP's security designation system is to confine offenders in the lowest security-level facility for which the offender qualifies, normally within 500 miles of the inmate's release residence.

But that doesn't always happen. Our team is firmly convinced that by understanding what's coming, it's easier for people to prepare for a successful journey.

Chapter 10

What Should I Know About Prison Transfers?

Based upon the number of minimum-security camps in the federal prison system, we estimate that less than 20% of the federal prison population gets the privilege of voluntarily surrendering. Being able to surrender to prison is a perk.

Ordinarily, when judges sentence people to serve less than 10-year terms, and the person does not have a history of violence or escape attempts, the Bureau of Prisons will classify that person as "minimum-security." Judges may allow those people to report to prison on their own volition. In the systems, it's known as "voluntary surrender."

There is an advantage to surrendering to prison voluntarily. It's less stressful. Rather than mixing with hundreds of other prisoners, many of whom may be intimidating, it's easier to have a family member or friend drive to the prison. A person walks in and presents himself to a guard. That's when the admissions process begins.

The other 80% of people that serve time do not get the privilege of voluntary surrender. They may have been held in detention centers for months because they did not qualify for release on bail. Or they may have been taken into custody right after the sentencing hearing.

In most cases, the U.S. Marshals service will transport those people to prison.

Prison offers comparatively more freedom than the local jail or detention center. But time in transit can be among the worst time a prisoner spends in confinement. For security reasons, staff members do not tell the prisoner when he is scheduled for transfer. That "unknown" factor brings considerable amounts of stress.

My partner, Michael, served 26 years in federal prisons of every security level. He transferred numerous times. In several of his books, including *Earning Freedom: Conquering a 45-Year Prison Term,* he wrote extensively about the transfer process.

Like everything else in confinement, there is a lot of hurry-up-and-wait. Once the officer notifies the prisoner to gather his belongings, the officer will rush the prisoner out of his area and lead him to a separate holding area, usually a cage or a room. The officer will lock the prisoner inside the new cage. If it's not full already, the cage where the prisoner is held will quickly fill with scores of other prisoners who also are being prepared for transfer. Think of a sardine can.

Occasionally, a jailer will come to the outside of the cage and scream for the prisoners to quiet down as he makes some announcement. The jailer will be looking for prisoners with special needs, medical and such, and provide instructions on what procedures will follow.

After the long wait—and a prisoner should expect to spend several hours as these preparations are made for transport—jailers will begin calling names, usually in groups of four or five. They will begin escorting those prisoners to another holding cell. Authorities will order the prisoners to strip naked as guards search for contraband.

The strip search is part of the journey. Guards will perform their visual inspections of naked prisoners several times during the transfer process. Although strip searches may humiliate a new prisoner, to guards it is routine and impersonal.

The prisoner strips naked. The guard stands about two feet in front of him and begins barking commands: "Lift your arms! Run your fingers through your hair! Open your mouth! Stick out your tongue! Lower your lips! Lift your genitals! Turn around! Let me see the bottom of your feet! Bend over! Spread 'em! Wider! Get dressed!"

After the strip search, the guard issues the prisoner a set of transfer clothing. The clothing is usually a one-size-fits-all set of bright orange overalls or elastic-waist paints.

Sometimes they include socks, other times not. The prisoner may get a pair of cloth slippers or rubber sandals, depending on what's available.

Guards will transfer the prisoner to another cell after he dresses in prison garb. He'll wait for every other prisoner being transferred to go through the same process. When the holding cell's noise reaches the same unbearable level, the prisoner will have a good indication that it will be time for the next procedure.

The next step is for guards to come around and begin locking the prisoners in chains. Prisoners will be called out of the cell, about three or four at a time.

A row of jailers will place steel cuffs around the prisoners' ankles, steel cuffs around the prisoners' wrists, and the guards will fasten the cuffs to a chain placed around each prisoners' waist. Once the prisoners are chained, they'll be led to yet another holding cage while they wait for all the other prisoners to join them.

After all the prisoners have been fastened in their traveling chains, guards will escort them to school-type buses. With steel bars covering the blacked-out windows, it's rather obvious the buses are used for prisoner transport. The prisoners march toward the buses, stumbling all the way because their ankles are chained together, moving slowly so the ankle chains don't dig too deeply into the skin around their ankles. The back of the bus has a caged area in which an officer rides, rifle in hand, to keep watch over the prisoners. When all prisoners are on board and accounted for, the bus departs.

Some prisoners are fortunate in that they are designated to prisons requiring only a single bus ride. Many, however, are designated to prisons far away and will take a combination of bus rides and plane rides as they make their long and arduous way to their respective institutions.

The U.S. Marshals operate a prisoner-transport service to move prisoners from coast to coast. The planes move in circular routes, and prisoners are scheduled to board these flights at the discretion of the U.S. Marshals and BOP administrators.

Consequently, moving from point A to point B may take 30 days or longer, with overnight stays in several facilities along the way—even if one is only transferring 100 miles. Thc circular route took one prisoner who was transferring from Fort Dix, New Jersey to Fairton, New Jersey (which is an hour away by car) on plane rides and bus rides through several states before delivering him.

What Makes Transfers Difficult:

Being transferred by the prisoner-transport service is difficult. The prisoner is in the dark and he never has an opportunity to settle in. Purchasing goods from the commissary may not be an option. The prisoner may be able to guess, but he'll never know how long he will remain in a particular facility. He may not have soap, toothbrush, or sandals to wear for the shower.

The more person knows about the process, and understands how to cope, the better prepared he will be. Our courses offer many interviews that show strategies that others have used to make it through challenging times.

A holdover prisoner in transit is the prison equivalent of a homeless person, living as a transient without any personal belongings. He is around strangers the entire time he's in transport, doesn't eat well, and is loaded with stress because he's out of touch with his family. The prisoner doesn't receive regular mail. He may have limited access to a quasi email system, which can somewhat ease the stress.

Besides a lack of access to personal property, and constant frustrations, the prisoner in transport is exhausted from all the middle-of-the-night wake-up calls, the waiting, the noise, the chains. In his book *Earning Freedom,* Michael wrote that time in transit was the worst part of his prison experience. He described strategies to keep a positive mindset.

Secondary Transfers:

After arriving at the designated facility, and progressing through the sentence, circumstances change. Sometimes it's possible to transfer to another facility.

Usually, prison transfers occur because of changes in the prisoner's security-level scoring. Other times prisoners may request transfers to similarly-rated facilities for their own reasons. Generally, case managers will not process a prisoner's request for transfer unless the individual has served at least 18 consecutive months of confinement in the institution with disciplinary-free conduct.

Even if an inmate meets the necessary criteria for transfer, his request to serve his sentence in a particular facility may or may not be granted. When a prisoner requests a transfer to a specific facility, he subjects himself to the discretion of administrators.

Ultimately, designators have the responsibility of controlling population levels in all of the federal prisons within his respective region. Consequently, a request to transfer to the FCI in Miami, Florida may result in a transfer to the FCI in Beaumont, Texas.

Prisoners may wonder whether there is anything they can do to enhance their chances of moving to a particular facility. Based on our extensive experience with the BOP, the formal answer is no. The informal answer is possibly. Everything is possible with self-advocacy.

In *Earning Freedom*, for example, Michael wrote about several instances where he was able to coordinate a "re-designation." On several occasions.

» Once, he was confined at the high-security prison in Atlanta. Authorities re-designated him to a medium-security prison in Oregon. He succeeded in blocking that transfer.

- » Later, effective self-advocacy led to his coordinating a transfer to McKean, in Northwest Pennsylvania.
- » While confined in a low-security prison in Fort Dix, New Jersey. Authorities moved to transfer Michael to a prison in Florida. He succeeded in getting that transfer reversed.
- » Much later in his sentence, he was serving time at the federal prison camp in Florence, Colorado. Authorities moved to transfer him to a camp in Texas. Effective self-advocacy helped him reroute his transfer to Lompoc, California.
- » Finally, he succeeded in coordinating a transfer from the camp in Taft to a camp in Atwater, to ease his preparations for release.

To succeed at coordinating transfers in a large bureaucracy, a prisoner must lay considerable amounts of ground work. Most people will not serve multiple decades in prison, and they will not encounter multiple transfers. On the other hand, for those that want to learn lessons in self-advocacy that will help them through the journey, we highly recommend our digital courses at ResilientCourses.com.

Influences on Prisoner Classification:

As anyone would expect, life in prison is different from anywhere else in America. There isn't as much liberty to influence outcomes. Everything is formulaic, with many policies and program statements that authorities follow. Those that master the policies may influence a smoother journey.

In 2018, President Trump signed the First Step Act. It's the first legislation that offers much in the way of incentives. According to that law, people in prison will have opportunities to participate in self-help programs. They will receive credit of sorts for that participation. Indeed, by participating, they will receive "Earned Time Credits" that will influence their classification status.

At the time we're writing this chapter, in the summer of 2019, the law is signed but the Bureau of Prisons has not fully implemented the Act. We anticipate the BOP will begin writing policies on the Act and begin implementing it completely in 2020. We will update our course as more information becomes available.

Prior to passage of the First Step Act, the federal system did not provide a means for prisoners to earn official recognition for constructive behavior.

In other words, a prisoner who was committed to developing skills and staying out of trouble could enhance his chances to succeed upon release.

Unfortunately, the classification system would not distinguish such people in any way from the prisoner that watched television and played cards all day.

Informally, some prisoners could establish chummy relationships with staff members, but on the record, only the BOP Custody Classification Form (BP-338) formally distinguished prisoners.

As the Custody and Classification Form showed, the BOP offered no vehicle for an individual to demonstrate that he was worthy of lower security through merit. BOP policy stated that a prisoner did not have a right to serve his term in a particular facility.

The only way for a prisoner's security level to drop would be through the passing of time and the avoidance of disciplinary infractions.

As a prisoner moved closer to his release date, his custody scoring may change for the better. Yet a prisoner did not have any control over the passing of time. Regardless of what personal accomplishments the individual achieved during his term in confinement, he did not have power to influence his security scoring positively.

We look forward to reviewing and writing about policy statements the Bureau of Prisons will publish on the First Step Act.

Our programs at ResilientCourses.com will include extensive coverage of those policies. We'll offer suggestions people going to prison may consider to get maximum benefit from the First Step Act, as our team interprets the polices.

But until the Bureau of Prisons publishes those policies, will rely upon the current policy statements. They do not differentiate a prisoner that adjusts positively from a prisoner that simply waits for calendar pages to turn.

As such, if a prisoner transferred or lost contact with the "informal" source of support he may have established with individual staff members, he would begin from square one. The Custody and Classification score will influence where he serves the sentence.

Although current policies do not offer much opportunities for people in prison to lower the classification score, federal prisoners have ample opportunities to demonstrate their need for higher security. Indeed, an individual's score would increase immediately if staff members found a person guilty of committing disciplinary infractions.

To avoid receiving disciplinary infractions, a prisoner must make a conscious effort. As some prisoners observed, trying to live in prison without receiving a disciplinary infraction was like trying to walk across a high wire—it's possible, but the feat requires concentration, balance, a strong will, and, above all, extraordinary discipline.

In prison, a person can control his own behavior. He cannot control the behavior of the thousands of other people with whom he lives. Nor can he control the whimsical moods and temperaments of staff members. They could charge a prisoner arbitrarily with violating any number of disciplinary infractions. The social interactions between other prisoners, as individuals and groups, require immediate and frequent decisions that could lead to disciplinary infractions.

Our team advises people to think about how every decision will influence their life in the next five minutes, the next five months, and the next five years.

A person can always minimize contact with volatile situations. Over multi-year periods, however, the odds of receiving a disciplinary infraction for violating some esoteric prison rule increase.

A person should beware of petty bureaucrats. Some people savor power they have over inmates and seem to aggressively look for opportunities to issue disciplinary infractions.

Those infractions may influence their careers in a positive way. That's not the case with all staff members, of course. But a person in prison would be wise to develop strong critical thinking skills, learning how and when to minimize exposure to volatility.

Although prisoners may misbehave in prison and cause their security levels to increase, in the past, "formal" channels did not exist for an inmate to enhance his chances of transferring to a more desirable facility. "Informal" methods, on the other hand, with varying degrees of acceptability, could be of assistance in requesting transfers to specific institutions.

We have hope that the First Step Act will bring positive changes. But until we read the BOP policy and program statements, we will reserve commentary on what people in prison should expect.

Initiating Transfer Requests:

The traditional path to initiate a transfer from one prison to another requires inmates to request their respective case manager to process the transfer paperwork. Usually, the case manager only will accept these requests for transfer during the regularly scheduled unit-team meeting (discussed in later modules).

If the inmate has 18 months of disciplinary-free conduct, and his security rating is consistent with the institution to which he wants to transfer, the case manager may agree to process the paperwork requesting a transfer. That paperwork gets routed to the unit manager, the case-manager coordinator, and then the warden for approval. If all parties agree to the transfer, staff members at the BOP's designation center in Grand Prairie, Texas will make the change.

Informal Influence on Classification:

Because the case manager, the unit manager, the case-manager coordinator, and the warden all must agree on the transfer before the request will proceed to assigned designator, some inmates try to develop close ties with these staff members. A few inmates who get along well with those staff members may find their requests to transfer successful. Others will not be so fortunate. Indeed, although staff members may tell the prisoner that a transfer request to a specific institution may or may not be granted, in reality, some staff members have influence. Those with influence can make a call to the regional designator and help an inmate's chances of being designated to a specific institution.

Outside Help:

Besides lobbying staff members from the local institution, a more aggressive approach may be to use outside resources. Those resources can lobby the regional designator, members of the U.S. Congress, and others that can influence the Bureau of Prisons.

Self-advocacy techniques, like phone calls and writing letters may be time-intensive and laborious, but as Michael wrote in *Earning Freedom*, they can prove effective in getting a positive outcome. Another option is to hire professional advocates or legal representation. But we urge caution when spending resources. Many organizations prey upon the vulnerable, making misrepresentations and promising outcomes that they do not have the power to deliver.

Chapter 11

What Should I Know About Staff Hierarchy?

Navigating the bureaucracy of prison requires at least a cursory knowledge of the key players and their roles. This section provides a basic overview to consider for those going inside.

Bureaucratic Structure:

Our nation incarcerates more people per capita than any other nation on earth. Millions of people have gone through the system, and thousands of people work in corrections. It's run like any other bureacracy, modeled in a hierarchical formation. The positions are more important than the individual, and the individuals rely upon program statements and policy statements to govern operations.

The organizational hierarchy is clearly defined and much more formal. Staff members that work alongside each other do not address each other with first names. Instead, we hear a lot "Mr." and "Ms," as if first names are offensive.

As stated previously, our team's experience is with The Federal Bureau of Prisons, which is organized under the Executive Branch of Government. For those that need a quick refresher course in civics, we have three branches of government in our country:

» The Legislative System: Divided by two houses of Congress, the Senate and the House. They pass laws all citizens must follow.

- » The Judicial System: Where judges interpret whether the laws have been applied appropriately.
- » The Executive Branch: Administrators and functionaries of the government.

The President of the United States leads the Executive Branch, and he appoints the Attorney General. On recommendation of the Attorney General, we have the *Director* of the Bureau of Prisons. The director oversees the BOP bureaucracy.

According to www.BOP.gov, in 2019 the federal prison bureaucracy includes 122 Bureau of Prisons facilities. Approximately 37,000 staff members oversee 184,000 people in prison. Obviously, such a huge system requires many rules and regulations. By adhering to those rules and regulations, they keep order. Those living inside can feel like cogs in a machine, without a common humanity.

The Regional System:

The BOP operates six regions, including:

1. Mid-Atlantic Region—prisons in West Virginia, Virginia, North Carolina, Maryland, Kentucky, and Tennessee
2. North Central Region—prisons in Illinois, Minnesota, Colorado, Kansas, Michigan, Wisconsin, Missouri, Indiana, and South Dakota
3. Northeast Region—prisons in Pennsylvania, Connecticut, New York, Massachusetts, Ohio, and New Jersey

4. South Central Region—prisons in Texas, Oklahoma, Arkansas, and Louisiana
5. Southeast Region—prisons in Georgia, Florida, Alabama South Carolina, Puerto Rico, and Mississippi
6. Western Region—prisons in California, Hawaii, Nevada, Arizona, Oregon, and Washington

Each region listed above has a single *Regional Director.* The regional director oversees policies and operations in each of the many institutions scattered around their respective territories. The various Directors of the Bureau of Prisons represent the highest levels of the BOP's Executive Staff. Few people in prison have any interaction with them.

Occasionally directors tour the facilities. When they do, local staff exert great efforts to shield those leaders from interactions with people serving time in prison. Prisoners can think of the directors as managing from the allegorical ivory tower. Although each director likely spent many years working in institutions, once they reach the pinnacle of the BOP bureaucracy, they isolate themselves from people that lower level staff members interact with on a daily basis.

Wardens:

Each institution has its own chief executive. In most cases this position is called *warden* in the staff hierarchy. During our team's extensive experience of serving time in prisons of every security level, we've been associated with multiple wardens. Each warden has his or her own management style.

The most effective wardens—from our perspective, manage by walking around. They make themselves available to talk with the people they're responsible for confining. Wardens in secure institutions stand around the cafeteria during the noon meal, which is the most popular meal in every prison.

A few times each month, they may visit camps that are adjacent to the secure prisons to make themselves to people classified as minimum-security. Wardens call it *standing mainline,* referring to the people that wait in the long lines for their daily meals. All prisoners are free to approach the warden, or any of the other staff members who stand mainline, to discuss a grievance or an issue of importance to the individual.

Many federal prisons are located within complexes that include several institutions of different security levels. Those complexes may have multiple wardens. Each institution has its own warden. But there would also be a complex warden, that oversees the entire complex. For example, the Federal Prison Complex in Colorado includes the following institutions:

- ADX Super-max Penitentiary
- USP High Security Penitentiary
- FCI Medium-Security Prison
- FPC Minimum-Security Prison

Florence includes one complex warden two wardens, and one camp supervisor.

Executive Assistant

An *Executive Assistant* serves each warden. More than anyone else, executive assistants shadow the warden. If a person approaches a warden, the executive assistant will listen to every word and possibly take notes. Few prisoners have any reason to interact directly with an executive assistant. The executive assistant is frequently the only staff member besides the warden who is authorized to speak with members of the media. Prisoners who interact with representatives of the media may have limited interactions with the executive assistant. For the most part, this isn't a staff member that will have much relevance to a person in prison.

Associate Wardens:

Most federal prisons hold in excess of 1,000 men. Some wardens are in control of institutions with more than 4,000 men and several hundred staff members. As the chief executive officers of these institutions, wardens have several colleagues beneath them on the organizational chart that manage various aspects of the prison.

In the prisons where we've been held, wardens rely upon associate wardens that concentrate on their own segments of the prison complex. Some typical associate warden positions include the following:

- » Associate Warden of Programs (AW-P)
- » Associate Warden of Industries and Education (AW-I&E)
- » Associate Warden of Operations (AW-O)
- » Associate Warden of Transportation (AW-T)
- » Associate Warden of Custody (AW-C)

The associate wardens, too, frequently stand mainline and make themselves available to speak with inmates who are concerned with departments under AW control. All members of the bureaucracy observe the clearly-defined chain of command, and associate wardens usually direct prisoners to seek assistance from staff members a bit lower in the bureaucratic hierarchy.

Department Heads:

Think of the prison as a miniature city, separated from the greater society by a series of boundaries. Just as in cities outside, the miniature prison city has various departments—like the department of housing, of health, and public works. In prison, the people leading these departments are department heads. Department heads report to their respective associate warden. Department Heads are much more immediately accessible to prisoners than higher members of the executive staff. Some of the Department Heads include:

» Unit Managers—One or more dormitory buildings comprise a housing unit, and the unit manager acts as a mini-warden over these units. He oversees matters related to inmate management, including the unit team (see below), each prisoner's central file, and each prisoner's release preparation.

» Supervisor of Education—In charge of administrating the education and recreational programs.

» Supervisor of Health Services—In charge of the medical and dental services.

» Captain—In charge of Lieutenants and custody staff.

» Supervisor of Food Services—In charge of the meal preparations.

» Supervisor of Facilities—In charge of maintaining the facility.

All department heads have a coterie of staff members that work beneath them. Those staff members interact directly with prisoners. Prisoners that have complaints against staff members are supposed to seek a resolution with the staff member first.

If they're not satisfied with the response they receive, the prisoners are supposed to work their way up the chain of command. If a grievance remains unresolved, prisoners have access to the *administrative remedy procedure* which we describe in the next module.

Unit Team:

With individual prisons holding well over a thousand men together, it would be impractical for the warden to know each of the prisoners under his control. Each federal prison, therefore, uses the Unit Management System. By assigning people to smaller, more manageable groups within the prison, the system keeps better control. The group of staff members with whom prisoners have the most frequent contact (except their immediate work-detail supervisor) are those who serve on their unit team.

On a typical prison compound (USPs, FCIs, and FPCs), the prisoners are free to mix in the general population. They eat in the same chow hall, participate in educational programs together, and share the same recreational facilities. Each inmate is assigned to a particular housing unit. Those housing units are restricted and considered off limits for people assigned to different housing units.

Each housing unit is led by a *Unit Manager.* The unit manager is a department head that presides over case managers and counselors—the other members of the

Unit Team. BOP Program Statement 5321.07 tells us that the unit team is also supposed to include an Education Advisor, and a Unit Psychologist. In our experience, those staff members have minimal interaction with people on the unit team.

Case Managers:

Case managers monitor progress of the prisoners assigned to their case load. They keep track of the prisoner's custody and classification scoring, his release date.

If the prisoner requests a transfer to another institution, the case manager is responsible for initiating this request. Every three years, or sooner if there is some change in the prisoner's status (transfer or nearing release), the case manager also prepares a *progress report*, which describes the prisoner's institutional adjustment.

When staff members activate programs within the First Step Act, case managers will document progress that prisoners make toward program completion.

Those completions will result in "Earned Time Credits," which they can redeem through various undefined incentive programs that should include transfer to home confinement.

Counselors:

Contrary to the title, counselors do very little in the way of counseling. Rather, their duties include overseeing the visiting lists and prisoner work details. They also may have a role in monitoring compliance with the Financial Responsibility Plan, assigning quarters, overseeing the sanitation of the unit, taking care of package mailouts, and participating on the Unit Disciplinary Committee.

Team Meetings:

People in prison that have more than two years remaining to serve are scheduled to meet with their unit team members twice each year. People with fewer than 24 months to serve meet with their unit team members more frequently. Usually, a person's unit manager, case manager, and counselor are present during these team meetings.

People in prisons shouldn't expect to learn much during these routine team meetings. Although rules may require attendance in team meetings, there is not much interaction or guidance with regard to what steps people can take to improve their status.

During the meeting, the case manager verbally reads for everyone present whatever documentation the unit team has accumulated since the previous team meeting. This documentation may include the person's work performance rating; his disciplinary record; his progress on the FRP plan; and whatever programs the individual has completed.

Newer people in the system may feel let down after a team meeting. They come into the meeting with hopes that they will find some meaning as to what they are supposed to be doing in prison. To many staff members, the only matters of importance include:

- The passing of time,
- The avoidance of disciplinary problems, and
- the payment schedule toward the FRP plan.

The counselor's function during the meeting is to describe a person's participation in the FRP program, and passes the prisoner a copy of his visiting list. The unit manager asks the prisoner whether he has any questions or requests. In most instances, the Team Meeting lasts fewer than 10 minutes.

Although the applicable Program Statement indicates that the:

> "Unit Manager is responsible for coordinating individual programs tailored to meet the particular needs of inmates in the unit," and that "such programming often is highly innovative and complex,"

Our team's experience has not shown that to be the case.

People that are determined to grow must become resourceful. They should become skillful at finding opportunities to do so on their own. They should anticipate some level of interference from staff members who view any type of activity that is "highly innovative and complex" as a threat to the status quo. As part of a large and complex law-enforcement bureaucracy, all prison systems revere uniformity.

Chapter 12

What Should I Know About the Administrative Remedy Process?

When people go into the prison system, our team encourages them to go in with their eyes wide open. When Michael began serving his sentence, back in 1987, he was 23 years old and didn't understand a thing. As a result of not understanding what would follow, he made a series of decisions during the earliest stages that complicated his journey.

Similarly, as explained in *Lessons from Prison*, Justin didn't have any idea about how prisons operated or what steps he could take to grow at the start. The more we know about the system, the more we empower ourselves to make good decisions, given the resources available to us.

We'd like to think that everything will proceed well. In reality, we're entering a system where things don't always go as we'd like. Sometimes, the atmosphere of imprisonment presents us with problems and challenges. It's not always within our power to change the situation, but we always have the ability to decide how we're going to adjust.

Problems within the system itself may complicate a person's life in prison. In the previous module, we offered a glance at the staff hierarchy that operates each prison.

If disputes arise, staff members prefer that we try to resolve them informally at the appropriate staff level. In other words, if a person has been assigned to a job that he didn't like, he shouldn't go complaining to the warden. An alternative may exist, like taking the grievance to the job supervisor or to the counselor.

When people cannot resolve grievances with a staff member, policy requires that they use the Administrative Remedy Process.

The Administrative Remedy Process offers staff members in the BOP an opportunity to review a prisoner's grievance. Sometimes the grievance is serious and a request for judicial relief is appropriate. But in most cases, people must exhaust their administrative remedy options before they can seek redress through the courts.

People in prison do not have a right to counsel through the Administrative Remedy Process. For that reason, they should learn how to prepare the grievance.

It's a plain-English complaint, but like everything else in prison, it's crucial to respect the process—complying with timelines and submitting the appropriate number of copies and so forth. In any prison, there will be people in the law library that would be willing to help file the grievance.

Informal Resolution:

The first step in the Administrative Remedy Process is called Informal Resolution. This step does not require paperwork, but it's wise to keep a journal, or notes of every step taken.

Staff members expect a person to make an attempt to resolve the matter with a simple conversation or request. If the problem persists, whatever it may be, the prisoner should then turn to his counselor for assistance.

The counselor will ask for an explanation and a description of efforts to resolve the problem informally. If the matter isn't resolved informally, the counselor should issue a BP-8 form, which is the first stage of the written procedure.

All of the forms are basic. The BP-8 requests a prisoner:

- » To state the problem,
- » To describe the efforts made to resolve the problem, and
- » To describe relief he seeks.

The form doesn't offer much space. Limit each request for remedy to one single issue. Keep a copy of the request because it will be necessary when filing the appeal. Once complete, pass the form to the counselor. The counselor should document attempts to resolve the matter, staff-to-staff. A person should expect a written response to his BP-8 from his counselor within a week.

BP-9:

If the response does not resolve the problem, and the individual wants to continue to the next stage in the process, the prisoner should request a BP-9. The BP-9 elevates the level of the grievance to the warden's level. It would be naïve to believe that the warden will review or even consider every grievance. Ordinarily, expect the warden to designate someone on his or her staff to respond to the BP-9 complaint. The warden may sign the response and the counselor will deliver a copy to the prisoner.

BP-10:

A prisoner who believes the warden has denied his request for relief inappropriately may pursue the matter to the next level through a BP-10 form. The counselor will provide the form.

The BP-10 is basically the same as the BP-9. It's an intermediate appeal that a person should send to the regional director. As with any other appeal, the prisoner can only raise issues the same issues that he presented to the warden. He is appealing the warden's decision, basically saying that the warden's response was wrong—in violation of the prison system's policies or in some way in violation of the prisoner's rights.

BP-10 Sensitive:

If the inmate is raising a complaint of a sensitive nature, like one that may involve the warden directly, or other staff members, the prisoner may request a "Sensitive BP-10." In this instance, the prisoner can file his request for administrative relief directly to the regional office. But the complaint must be truly sensitive to pursue this route.

BP-11:

Finally, if a person doesn't receive the relief requested from the regional director, he may file a BP-11. This is the last stage of the administrative-remedy process. Prisoners should send their BP-11, with supporting documentation, to the BOP headquarters in Washington, DC.

Procedures:

Bureaucratic procedures require people in prison to file their grievances in a timely manner. If they miss deadlines, staff members will move to dismiss the complaints as being out of time.

- » BP-9: Must file within 20 days following the date on which the basis for the request occurred.
- » BP-10: Must file within 20 days following the date on which the warden returned his response.
- » BP-11: File with the general counsel at BOP Headquarters within 30 days of the date that he received the response from the regional director.

Rules permit people in prison to assist each other on all legal matters.

After exhausting the administrative process, if the person continues to feel as if the prison system is violating his rights, he may file a complaint in the federal district court.

We advise people to choose their battles carefully. When it comes to military strategy, a wise general willingly loses a few battles for the higher goal of winning the war. We can learn from military strategists. If a person in prison expects to experience some discomfort, he may have a higher tolerance and strong enough mindset to let some grievances slide.

Discretion and Critical-Thinking:

Staff members form close relationships with each other. They can easily prevail upon their relationships with colleagues to make life uncomfortable for a person in prison. People that develop reputations for filing frivolous (or not so frivolous) complaints can make a bad situation worse. They can lose access to visiting, to telephone, to email. Staff members may lock a person in Special Housing for an administrative investigation. They may transfer a person across state lines.

It's crucial to remember that when judges sentence people in federal court, they say:

» "I hereby sentence you to the custody of the attorney general."

At that point, from the system's perspective, the person has become an inmate. BOP staff members have enormous discretion. **They have enormous power over the life of a human being.**

For this reason, we advise people to go through prison *as a submarine.* We want them to travel beneath the surface, avoiding problems at all costs. Like a submarine, keep the periscope up to know what's going on in the area. But be silent and safe, avoiding problems with both staff and others. Avoiding complications is the best way to get through a prison term successfully.

Our team advises people to use discretion and critical-thinking skills when it comes to filing a request relief through the Administrative Remedy Process. Prison is different from the judicial system.

Rights to discovery do not exist and people in prison do not have a right to cross examine accusers or witnesses during the administrative-remedy process. In some cases, it's necessary to file administrative remedy procedures in order to advance to the federal judicial system. But more often than not, administrative-remedy is a losing proposition and it's best to let the grievance slide.

In our online course, we offer commentary and analysis of administrative remedy processes that have gone wrong and that have gone right.

Chapter 13

What Should I Know About The Disciplinary Code?

It would be best to avoid problems while in prison. But as described throughout this book, that isn't always easy. Depending upon security levels, complexities surface.

People in prison must interact with hundreds, or thousands of people. Some of those people have mental health issues. Some of those people have an agenda that differs from a person that wants to focus on getting out of prison at the soonest possible time, with the least amount of trouble.

It's a reason we believe that every person going into the system should learn as much as possible. To get the outcome they want, they must always use critical-thinking skills, understanding ramifications that may come with every decision.

The BOP considers all employees correctional officers first. Any staff member, including secretaries, cooks, chaplains, and landscapers have the authority to write a disciplinary infraction.

In federal prison, the informal name for infractions are "*shots.*" When a prisoner receives an infraction, it's known as getting a shot. Many state prison system refer to those infractions as "tickets."

The BOP publishes its detailed disciplinary codes in Title 28 of the Code of Federal Regulations, §541.

BOP Program Statement 5270 also includes the disciplinary code.

Whenever a person comes into an institution, staff members will issue him a handbook that details all prohibited acts.

There are four levels of prohibited acts, categorized as:

» Greatest (100 series),

» High (200 series),

» Moderate (300 series), and

» Low-Moderate (400 series).

Each prohibited act is given a number, and those with the lowest numbers, the 100-series acts, are the most serious.

They include infractions like murder, rioting, drug dealing, rape, and other violent acts. 200-series acts include violations like stealing, fighting, and drinking. 300-series shots are much more common, and include violations like having contraband, being out of bounds, and disobeying a direct order. 400-series shots are rather minor, like being late for work or running a business inside the prison. For example, if one person tries to earn a little money by charging someone for laundry services or some other routine activity in the underground economy, he may receive a 400-series shot, or a 300-series shot for "running a business."

According to BOP policy, a staff member who chooses to write a disciplinary infraction must file the shot within 24 hours of the time that the staff member became aware of the incident. If there are exceptional circumstances, the staff member may delay. But that delay could be grounds for the person to appeal, if it is out of time.

Usually, staff members who write shots deliver them to the Lieutenant's Office for an initial review. Once the lieutenant considers the written report, the lieutenant calls the prisoner into the office.

The lieutenant reads Miranda rights ("You have the right to remain silent," and on and on) because it's a quasi-legal proceeding. Then, the lieutenant will read the contents of the shot. The lieutenant will ask the person whether he wants to make a statement. He will ask whether the person wants to call any witnesses.

If the prisoner intends to contest the infraction, he must be aware of the procedures. The only opportunity he will have to call a witness will be at this "investigation" stage. If he fails to call a witness, or present any other exculpatory evidence at this stage, staff members may refuse to consider the evidence later. Silence, incidentally, likely will lead a lieutenant and others to infer guilt.

If the shot is serious in nature (a 100- or 200-series shot), the prisoner will be placed in handcuffs and taken to the Segregated Housing Unit (SHU—see below for description) directly after receiving the shot. For 300- series shots, the prisoner may or may not be taken to the Special Housing Unit. With 400-series shots, the prisoner generally will be released to the prison compound to await further proceedings.

Unit Disciplinary Committee:

Representatives from a person's Unit Team, ordinarily, are supposed to call the prisoner for a Unit Disciplinary Committee Hearing (UDC) within 72 hours from the time that the lieutenant processed the shot (not counting weekends or holidays). The UDC is the first stage of a court proceeding.

Case managers or unit managers on the UDC are authorized to provide a hearing for 300- and 400-series infractions. The UDC may also dispense sanctions for these low and moderate infractions. The sanctions may include loss of telephone, visiting, commissary, or a combination of privileges.

During that UDC hearing, a counselor, case manager, and or unit manager will listen to the prisoner's version of events. They will then make a finding—guilty or not guilty.

People that proceed through the UDC should not expect the same level of due process that exists in court. Theoretically, the judicial system is based on a presumption of innocence until proven guilty. In prison, that presumption of innocence does not exist.

Indeed, prison disciplinary hearings are as close to the infamous kangaroo court as is known in America. Prisoners may not cross-examine their accusers; they have no rights to discovery; and since prison administrators must maintain the order of their institutions, the word of a staff member is given more weight than the word of a prisoner.

Prisoners should expect the UDC to find them guilty if a staff member writes a shot. They may appeal the shot through the Administrative Remedy Procedure.

Disciplinary Hearing Officer:

If the prisoner receives a serious shot of the 100- or 200-series level, he must appear before the Disciplinary

Hearing Officer (DHO). All infractions involving the telephone, too, must go before the DHO.

The DHO hearing is like the UDC hearing, but punishments are much more severe. Rather than losing simple privileges, the DHO may sentence a prisoner to segregation for several months at a time.

A DHO may take away telephone, visiting, and commissary privileges for ten-year terms (or longer). He may extend a person's stay in prison by taking away accrued good time.

No corporal punishment exists in today's prison system, but there is no shortage of psychological punishments at the DHO's disposal. People that violate laws may be referred to the FBI for prosecution, too.

Summary:

1. Shots begin when a staff member writes a formal infraction and files the disciplinary infraction with the Lieutenant's office.
2. A lieutenant reviews the shot, then calls for the prisoner to appear before him. The lieutenant provides the prisoner with his only opportunity to make a statement or present evidence that could lead to further "investigation" by the lieutenant.
3. In most cases, the lieutenant will refer the shot to the Unit Disciplinary Committee, and those on the committee will adjudicate the shot.
4. The prisoner may or may not be taken to segregation immediately upon the issuance of the shot, depending on its seriousness.

5. And prisoners should be aware that it may be easier to find a four-leaf clover in a field of hay than to overturn a disciplinary infraction once a shot has been written.

Collateral Effects of Disciplinary Infractions:

Besides bringing immediate sanctions, disciplinary infractions adversely influence a person's Custody and Classification score. The form used to compute a prisoner's security level takes credit away for any disciplinary reports received within the past year. Disciplinary infractions at the 200-series level count against an individual for two years. Disciplinary infractions at the 100-series level count against an individual for ten years.

Further, if an individual is found guilty of fighting, the BOP will consider him a violent offender. That distinction will adversely influence his custody scoring for the remainder of time he is confined. Again, few opportunities exist for a prisoner to distinguish himself positively, there is no limit to the number of ways he can make his time in prison more onerous.

Segregated Housing Unit (SHU):

The Segregated Housing Unit (SHU), also known as *"the hole,"* usually is contained in its own building within the prison fences. Although I was fortunate to have avoided any time in SHU during the time when I was held at Taft camp, my partner and co-author, Michael spent several months in SHU during the 300+ months that he lived as a prisoner. Further, I've interacted with many clients that were transferred to SHU for administrative reasons. From all of them, I've learned a great deal about what it's like. If we think of prison as a miniature city, we can think of SHU as the equivalent of a county jail.

When staff members send people to SHU, the prisoners lose access to many of the privileges available in the general population. Those in SHU, for example, are restricted to their closet-sized rooms for 23- to 24-hours each day. Sometimes they are alone. More often than not, they're crammed into crowded conditions. They may be locked in the small quarters with one or two other prisoners (one may have to sleep on the floor).

Staff may limit SHU prisoners to the quantity of showers they may take—usually three per week; they may be limited to one clothing change per week; they may be limited to one hour of recreation per day. And recreation means that they're transferred from their cell to another cell with fresh air; they have limited access to mail, reading materials, telephone, and commissary.

Time in SHU exacerbates the pains of imprisonment. Some prisoners who remain in SHU for prolonged periods of time sometimes complain of becoming disoriented. There are few opportunities to interact with others. It's difficult to escape the noise that others generate. Many people try to relieve their boredom of being locked in the small rooms by banging on the doors or yelling through the spaces in the door jamb to others on *lockdown*. Some seek attention by stuffing their clothing into the toilets, then repeatedly flushing the toilet to flood the tier. It's a pathetic attempt to frustrate the guards and garner attention.

In *Earning Freedom*, Michael wrote that he maintained a positive mindset in SHU by both writing and exercising. Although the room was smaller than a walk-in closet, he said that he could run for hours in the cell, going from one end to the other. He could set goals by doing pushups or other exercises. As human beings, we can adjust anywhere, even in closed quarters.

SIS Investigation:

As I've learned from many clients, staff members may send people to the SHU for any number of reasons. The obvious reason is as a sanction for having been found guilty of violating a disciplinary rule. A less coherent reason is for "investigation."

Each prison has its own Special Investigative Services (SIS) lieutenant. The SIS operates as a kind of FBI agency, or group of detectives within the prison. They may launch investigations for suspected violations of prison rules or policies.

The SIS investigates wrongdoing, or suspected wrongdoing, among inmates and staff. SIS lieutenants may learn of activities they want to investigate through any number of methods, including *"shakedowns"* of personal property that result in incriminating evidence.

SIS lieutenants get their information from a variety of sources, including people in the population. In order to get some type of personal benefit, many people tell staff members about the activities of others. For example, someone may talk with staff about:

- » A person that operates a gambling pool;
- » A group of prisoners who are extorting weaker people;
- » A person that takes food from the kitchen and sells to others in the housing unit; or
- » A person may talk about staff members that have romantic relationships with people in pris-

on, or staff members that bring contraband into the institution.

Such information may result in an SIS investigation. The SIS may place suspected prisoners under *administrative detention* (AD) until the investigation is complete.

The SIS may hold a person in AD for several months. While under the AD status, people live quite similarly to those who are being punished for having been found guilty of committing disciplinary infractions. They have less liberty, and less access to telephones, books, radios, and other property.

Besides investigations, staff may hold people in the AD ward of the SHU for a number of other reasons. One reason may be a person's request. Some people feel so threatened in the general population that they choose *protective custody* (PC) and they voluntarily live under the more spartan conditions of SHU.

Staff may keep people in the SHU until more room becomes available in the general population, or until they get more information regarding classification. It is unfortunate, but in some cases, a person gets to the prison before his PSR or other paperwork arrive. When that happens, out of an abundance of caution, staff members may put the individual in SHU until they get clarity on his classification.

Final Word:

Like any large and growing bureaucracy, the Bureau of Prisons is a highly structured organization. It is exceptionally impersonal. People should prepare themselves mentally for the challenges that accompany confinement. As we've written before, it's 100 times more bureaucratic than other government agencies, like the IRS or DMV. Awareness of how the system operates can lead to better decisions, and the avoidance of disciplinary problems.

Despite the rigidity, opportunities for growth exist. In order to harness those opportunities, our team recommends that people make themselves aware of every rule. Learn how to navigate rules like a skier slaloms a course down a snow-covered mountain.

In our course, we offer more insight into stories of people that went through prison and emerged successfully. Anyone that chooses a disciplined, deliberate path can do the same.

Chapter 14

What Should I Know Before Being Admitted to Prison?

Michael and I got to prison in different ways. Authorities charged Michael with violating laws related to drug trafficking. Those charges carried the possibility of multiple decades in prison.

As he wrote in *Earning Freedom,* authorities confined him from the day that they arrested him. He started in detention centers, and then U.S. Marshals transported him to prison.

My charges, on the other hand, related to violating securities laws. As a result of those charges being "white collar" in nature, I surrendered to prison voluntarily—and never saw a pair of handcuffs until the day that I began serving my sentence.

Not all people convicted of white collar offenses get surrender to prison voluntarily. But as far as our team can tell, all people get to prison in one of two ways.

Those classified with minimum-security may be able to report individually—known as self-surrendering. As described in earlier sections, it's an advantage for several reasons. As an immediate benefit, people that surrender voluntarily don't get thrown into the crowded and dehumanizing mix of the prison transit system.

Another benefit with self-surrendering is that it confirms a federal judge did not see the person as a threat. Prison officials give consideration to the judge's discretion. When assessing, or classifying prisoners that self-surrender, BOP officials give credit that results in a lower score on the custody and classification system.

Most people get to prison through some type of prisoner transport system like the one Michael described. In the federal system, the US Marshals transports people to prison. Although there is no easy way to report for confinement, those who have the privilege of turning themselves in experience a lot less frustration and humiliation.

Thoughts on Self-Surrendering:

Unless a person has a valid reason to postpone the surrender date, it may be best to start serving the sentence as quickly as possible. Intuitively, many people want to postpone their surrender date.

In our accompanying course, available at ResilientCourses.com, we offer many examples of successful journeys through prison. Members of our team have real depth and breadth of experience. I've worked with more than 1,000 people that have self-surrendered. As an attorney, our partner Shon has worked on sentencing memorandums for more people than he can count. And Michael has written about and interviewed more than 1,000 people that have gone into the prison system.

Our personal experience convinces us that unless there is a valid reason, it's best to surrender to get started in prison at the soonest possible time.

From the time a person becomes a target of a criminal investigation, it feels as if the person is serving time. The criminal charge interrupts an ability to earn a living. It disrupts the family and social life. It's as if the person is serving time, but the time is not counted toward satisfying the sentence.

Our team has worked with people that repeatedly request the judge to postpone the surrender date. Sometimes there are valid reasons to postpone a surrender date. For example, a person may have family or business complications to resolve.

Judges have discretion to suspend the surrender date. For some people with whom we've worked, judges postponed a surrender date by several years. Through our courses and consulting practice, we teach from those stories.

On the other hand, we've worked with many people that postpone their surrender to prison simply because they want to procrastinate. Those people serve time without the time counting toward the sentence. They can't get their life together. Once they do get to prison, they realize that their fear of the unknown was the worst part. They adjust. On the other side of the journey, when they're counting the days to be released, they always wish that they had surrendered earlier. Some realize that they wasted time by postponing their surrender.

Every case is personal and individual. In some cases, it's best to rip the band aid off and start the process of healing with an early surrender date. For people without financial resources, we recommend getting to prison as quickly as possible. Those that have complicated businesses to operate may have valid reasons to postpone their surrender.

Getting Designated:

After the judge imposes sentence, a designator for

the Bureau of Prisons will assign the individual to report to a particular prison. BOP policy states that:

> individuals ordinarily will be placed in prisons with the lowest classification rating for which the prisoner is eligible within 500 miles of his residence.

Those that want to see the locations of all federal prisons may visit www.BOP.gov.

The system is crowded. It may not always be possible for the BOP to designate a person to serve the sentence in an institution within 500 miles of the person's residence.

- » Some regions have fewer prisons than other regions.
- » Some people may want to participate in programs that are only available in prisons outside of the region.
- » Some people may need specialized medical care that is only available outside of the region.

The First Step Act includes a provision regarding this 500-mile guideline. And people may be able to participate in programs, or advocate for themselves to influence a transfer to a specific prison. But it's important to remember that judges sentence people "To the custody of the Attorney General," BOP officials have enormous discretion with regard to where a person serves the sentence.

If a judge authorizes a person to self-surrender, but traveling to the prison is too costly, the person has the the option of accepting free transportation through the prisoner transport system. If the option is available, our team recommends surrendering voluntarily to prison. Avoid traveling in chains and steel cuffs if given the option.

Bringing Items into the Prison:

If self-surrendering is an option, people may want to know what they can bring with them. With few exceptions, the short answer is nothing other than medical necessities and identification.

Rules in the BOP apply to all facilities. Yet wardens have enormous discretion. Some wardens or staff members may authorize a person to enter the prison with sneakers, athletic apparel, medication, religious articles, wrist watches, radio, or other personal items of limited value. In our experience, however, prisons prefer people to surrender without any personal items.

Those that want clarification from the prison where they're going may want to call for clarification before surrendering. They also may download an inmate handbook from the prison by visiting the BOP website for more clarity [See BOP (dot) gov if you have Internet access].

Although the prison system provides the necessities for an individual to survive, it also offers access to a commissary. People with financial resources may purchase various items to ease the burdens of confinement. As with anywhere else in America, people with financial resources may have an easier adjustment.

Prisoners have a right to keep legal documents in limited amounts. For that reason, it may make sense to write important phone numbers, addresses, and other information on a page and place that page in an envelope marked "Legal Material." Bring that material to the prison when surrendering. It may also make sense to put the information in a self-addressed envelope and place it in the mail the day before surrendering. This information will prove valuable when settling into the prison and setting up approved lists for phone calls, visits, and emails.

Besides considering money and legal documents, consider any information from a physician that documents medical conditions. If a person is taking prescriptions, it would be wise to consult the formulary on the BOP website. The formulary will show all medications that the BOP authorizes. If the medication is not listed on the BOP formulary, it may be wise to ask a physician for a different prescription that complies with the formulary. It may also be wise to bring a 30-day supply of medication to the prison.

If an individual suffers from a bad back, from weak knees, or from any ailment that prevents the individual from specific work details, from climbing stairs, or from climbing to a top bunk, get a letter from a physician. It's best to document medical conditions in the PSR. Letters from doctors can also prove helpful. Think about steps to coordinate these letters that may be helpful prior to surrendering to prison.

Prisons usually allow people to keep their eyeglasses with them when they report. Once inside the system, however, it may not be so easy to replace the eyeglasses. Those who wear eyeglasses ought to check the prison policy before they report. Ideally, they should bring two pair of durable eyeglasses with them. A spare set of eyeglasses will help a person if the primary set loses a screw or breaks.

Create a Contact Plan:

Whether a person surrenders to prison voluntarily, or arrives via a law enforcement transport system, the first step will be to go through the admissions process. That process may take several hours. It's a good idea to let a family member, friend, or attorney know that they should expect a call within 24 hours of surrendering.

Even if a person doesn't get immediate access to a telephone, he should be able to ask another person in prison to make a call to someone that can relay a message. The message should be basic: "I'm fine and I will call within a few days, or as soon as I can access the phone."

If the contact person does not receive the message, it may be because authorities locked the individual in the SHU upon arrival. On occasion, that happens because the person arrives at the prison before appropriate paperwork arrives. If no one checks on the paperwork—including the PSR, Statement of Reasons, and Judgment order—the person may languish in the SHU for several weeks.

People should have an advocacy plan in place in the event that contact is not made with the support group within a day or two. Their loved ones or attorneys would be in a better position to make inquiries with the BOP to resolve the matter. A person in prison may not have access to a telephone if he is in the SHU.

Being Processed Inside:

The first stop for people being admitted to prison is the Receiving and Discharge (R&D) Department. Moving through R&D is like a booking procedure. If the person has been arrested before, he will find the process familiar. Sometimes a person will be processed through R&D in fewer than two hours. Other times the booking process can take a full day. Everything depends upon staff availability and the number of people being processed at a given time.

If a person surrenders in the morning voluntarily, he may be the only person being processed. In that instance, he could be on the prison compound before lunch. If a person arrives on a bus with 50 other people, he may not get to the compound for eight hours or longer.

Officials will lock the prisoner inside of a holding cell that is consistent with his security score. People that have been classified as minimum-security will be held in separate holding cells from people that are going into adjacent, higher-security prisons.

Once staff members lock people in the appropriate holding cells, they pass out many intake forms. Each person will need to complete the intake forms, and they become a part of the individual's *Central File*.

The central file follows the person throughout the term in the BOP. It includes the PSR and the Judgment order provided by the court. Over the duration, staff members add various forms and reports that document progress.

The case manager keeps the central file in order. People have a right to review the contents of the central file, and generally may do so after submitting a written request to the case manager.

Intake forms ask the individual to identify whom the BOP should contact in case of death or emergency. They offer insight into a person's medical history. Other forms provide consent for the person to receive mail and they confirm that the person received a copy of the "Inmate Handbook."

The handbook details all of the rules, rights, and responsibilities of every person in the prison. By confirming receipt of the handbook, the person immediately becomes responsible for adhering to the rules and regulations.

If a person doesn't follow the rules, authorities will subject him to the code of disciplinary proceedings. For that reason, those that have access to the Internet should review inmate handbooks available for download through the BOP website, or through our courses at ResilientCourses.com.

Besides filling out many forms, staff members will take a new mug shot of every incoming prisoner. They will record his fingerprints. They will strip search him. They will provide him with a new set of clothing. In most cases, prisoners have a choice of mailing home the clothing they wore into the institution or donating it to the prison. Prisoners who arrive at a prison wearing their own clothing would be wise not to wear anything they particularly value.

» In *Lessons from Prison,* I described intake procedure in detail. Get a free copy of *Lessons from Prison* by visiting ResilientCourses.com.

Before moving a person from R&D to the next station in the admissions journey, a series of staff members will interview each new prisoner. After reviewing the central file, a case manager will ask the prisoner whether there is any reason he feels he would be in danger if he were to mix with the general population. That may be an intimidating question. A response may be institution specific. Obviously, minimum-security camps and low-security prions have very low levels of volatility. Medium- and high-security prisons will be more volatile.

People that fear for their safety do not have many options. If they have a valid reason, they may ask to check into *protective custody* (PC). PC is an area of the Segregated Housing Unit where inmates are kept locked in their cell for 23 hours each day and isolated from others. The living conditions and privileges are much more spartan than in the general population. Relatively few people in prison choose this option.

Besides case managers, a representative from Health Services will interview each person in the holding cell. They will review the PSR and any medical records to determine whether the person has any special medical needs.

Staff members from psychology and the custody departments may also ask questions. A counselor may also speak with the person before processing him into the system.

Identification (ID) Card:

Once the Receiving and Discharge department processes the person, an officer will give each person his identification card. The ID includes the mug shot and registration number. People in prison are supposed to have the ID card with him any time he leaves the housing unit. If a person loses the card, staff will charge him a fee to replace it. Being without an ID card may result in a disciplinary infraction.

Admissions and Orientation (A&O) Unit:

People that go to minimum-security prisons will

ordinarily go directly to the camp. Those going to low-, medium-, or high-security prisons may go to unit reserved for new prisoners.

They may remain in that Admissions and Orientation Unit for several days or weeks while they await placement assignment to more permanent housing quarters.

While in the A&O unit, prisoners become acquainted with the prison routine. They usually are not assigned permanent jobs or quarters until after they have completed the A&O program. A&O prisoners may or may not mix with the general population outside of the unit, in the chow hall, in the recreation areas, library, or any common areas besides the individual housing units.

It's a good idea to use time in the A&O unit to gather information about routines and resources available in the prison.

Callout Sheet:

Every federal prison publishes a daily printout, the *Callout Sheet*. The callout sheet is like a schedule of events. All people in prison have a responsibility to check the callout sheet daily. It lets the person know whether he is required to report to various departments at a given time.

The callout sheet is available in the same place every day, usually by the unit officer's desk. The callout sheet lists names in alphabetical order with the prisoner's registration number. It includes the time and location of all appointments. Staff members publish callout sheets Monday through Friday, except holidays, after the daily 4:00 p.m. census count.

If the callout sheet lists an appointment—known as a callout—and the person fails to report, a staff member may write a disciplinary infraction, accusing the person of being out of bounds for missing the callout. During the A&O process, prisoners generally have callouts every day.

Admissions and Orientation Program:

In the federal system, all prisoners must participate in an A&O Program. This involves a series of lectures that take place over a day or two. A specific person, like a counselor, is usually assigned to coordinate the A&O program. He coordinates staff members from various departments that come speak with the people in A&O. People may ask questions during A&O, but we've found it best to remain silent and listen. It's best to get information from other people that are living in the world of confinement and get out of A&O as quickly as possible.

Be cautious about asking too many questions during A&O. Although people may be curious, it's generally not a best-practice technique to questions in a public forum. Those questions give away personal information to an experienced prisoner. Some prisoners will spread rumors, and information can prove toxic to a person's reputation in prison. Remember the submarine metaphor. Be silent and aware while going through prison.

Prior to going through the A&O process, inmates will get a handbook which includes all rules, regulations, and information concerning the operation of the prison. People in prison should study the handbook closely. They may find details that can prove helpful during the adjustment process.

Final Word:

After prisoners complete the A&O program, they become a part of the general prison population.

Our team likes to quote a study by Stanton Wheeler a criminologist. Dr. Wheeler suggested that prisoners come into the system with values that closely resemble the society they left behind.

As prisoners move deeper into their sentences, the prisoners gradually pull away from the values of that society. They become more familiar with prison culture and adapt to the world inside. The men become *"prisonized,"* so to speak. They begin using the vernacular that exists in the fences and participating in activities that they otherwise would not consider.

As the prisoner passes beyond the halfway point of his sentence, and starts moving closer to release, the criminologist suggested that prisoners go through another value shift. They move back in line with behavior acceptable in the society he left behind.

Wheeler suggested that prisoners adapt according to this U-shaped curve. Society outside of fences is above the "U" and society inside the fences is below the "U." Stanton Wheeler published his study in 1961, but I find it just as valid today. All prisoners, theoretically, move through the U.

After the prisoner leaves the A&O Unit and joins the general prison population, he must adapt to this abnormal society.

The prisoner will have to make choices from options that do not exist in the world outside of fences. Ramifications follow those choices. Dilemmas present themselves every day.

- » Do I respond to problems in a manner that is appropriate for the society in which I live outside of prison?
- » Do I respond to problems in a manner that is appropriate for the prison society in which I now reside?
- » What are the ramifications of each decision I make?

Although every prisoner can control his own behavior, he cannot control the behavior of the thousands of other people serving time alongside him. In order to survive the sentence with minimal aggravation, and to grow through it, prisoners need a strong mind and a sense of balance.

Our team and the lessons we provide in our courses at ResilientCourses.com offer enormous insight. We highly recommend that people learn from those courses to prepare for best outcomes.

A model inmate (from the vantage point of prison administrators) is one who abides by every prison rule, who holds a full-time job—preferably in the prison factory—and asks for nothing outside the ordinary. Our experience, however, suggests that people in prison should strive for something more.

Rather than offering a "how-to-live-in-prison course," we teach people how to get best outcomes. People should use time in prison to prepare for successful lives upon release. Members of our team did not only make it through prison successfully, we got out of prison and built successful careers. Anyone can do the same if they learn to make values-based, goal-oriented decisions. We're confident our courses can help people get best outcomes.

The following chapters offer basics about living in prison and navigating obstacles. We offer vignettes with hopes of both teaching and inspiring people. Prison is different. Learn how to master it with courses we make available at ResilientCourses.com.

Chapter 15

How Does Housing Differ by Security Levels?

As revealed in earlier modules, my experience of living in prison is limited to the time that I served at the Taft Federal Prison Camp.

My friend, partner, and co-author, Michael Santos, however, taught me a great deal about the prison system. He served time in prisons of every security level. Through working with him and with our clients, I've developed a level of understanding about living in other prisons. Through ResilientCourses.com, we offer an abundance of information to prepare people for every type of prison experience.

All prison systems use scoring mechanisms to determine the level of security that is appropriate. Those with documented histories of violence, escape attempts, and long sentence lengths may be more likely to serve terms in higher security prisons.

Those without histories of violence, escape attempts, and relatively shorter sentences may serve their sentences in lower-security prisons.

Again, our team members have experience in prisons of every security level. We've learned that regardless of where authorities place an individual, opportunities exist to grow and prosper. Success in prison, and anywhere else, starts with having a strong mindset. It's also helpful to understand more about the journey ahead.

For most people confined to larger prisons, the journey begins inside of a housing unit reserved for people going through the Admissions and Orientation program. After prisoners complete all requirements of A&O, administrators reclassify them and transfer them to one of the general housing units.

Smaller prisons may not have space for a separate A&O section. In smaller prisons, staff members assign people to general population as soon as they arrive. As a general rule, prisoners are assigned to regular quarters in the first weeks of their confinement. Exceptions might occur in certain crowded penitentiaries, where inmates wait in segregation or the A&O unit for weeks or months at a time before quarters become available.

Eventually, prisoners can expect to mix with others in the general population—unless staff members consider the person a threat to security. When that happens, they may isolate the person indefinitely.

We consider two aspects of prison life critical:

1. Quarters assignment, and
2. Job assignment

Authorities have discretion on where they assign a person to sleep and work. Those decisions can influence a person's adjustment. If a person is forced to share a housing assignment with someone that doesn't interact well with others, problems can occur. Risk escalates quickly and dramatically. This is equally true when a person has to work alongside someone who is full of hatred. There isn't any shortage of hatred in the prison system.

U.S. Penitentiaries and Medium-security FCIs:

Living quarters in federal prison depends upon the security level of the institution. United States Penitentiaries and medium-security Federal Correctional Institutions both hold high-security prisoners. Many of the people in those prisons serve sentences of multiple decades, or life terms. They may have long histories of violence, gang affiliation, and disruption. In response, staff members enforce rules and procedures that limit movement. They want to keep order.

The housing units in most USPs and FCIs include two-man rooms. The rooms are spartan. As a rule, they measure about eight-feet -by- ten-feet, the size of a small bathroom. The walls are concrete cinder block. Floors will be an unfinished concrete, with a freestanding toilet and sink made of brushed aluminum. The toilet will not have a seat or lid.

The room will not have a view and may not have a window at all. If the room has a window, the frosted glass will be non-transparent and will not open. Windows will be so narrow that a grown man's head could not pass through them.

The rooms will have a bunk-bed frame made of steel tubing and steel sheets that are attached to the wall. Each prisoner will be assigned a thin mat to place on the rack for sleeping. Everything about the room is hard. There will be no wood in the cell, no soft colors. It's all steel and concrete. Cold. Austere, like the entire prison.

Prisoners can expect two small lockers that hold all the personal belongings of the men assigned to the room. The lockers are just under four-feet high and about two-feet wide. No personal belongings are allowed to be left outside of the lockers between 7:30

a.m. and 4:00 p.m. Disregarding this rule may result in a trip to segregation.

Most people want to avoid unnecessary trips to SHU. While they are in the hole, they do not have access to their property, to the relative freedom of movement, or to other privileges, like the telephone and clothing exchanges. Further, some penitentiaries are so crowded that when one is sent to the hole even for a trivial shot, he may have to wait three months before another space becomes available in the prison's general population.

Prison rules forbid the men from hanging photographs or anything else on the wall. One fluorescent light is attached to the ceiling, and a smaller light may be above the sink. The room may have a steel plate bolted to the wall, with an attached swivel stool. Penitentiary rooms are monastic, not conducive to writing or creativity.

The rooms have thick steel doors with a narrow window. Staff members peer into the room routinely, so the windows cannot be blocked, even when an occupant is using the toilet. There is no expectation of privacy in prison. At any time, a staff member may come into the room and rifle through one's property. They have a right to search for contraband, or weapons that prisoners may manufacture.

A few feet above floor level, the steel doors have a cut-in slot with a small trap door. When the cellblock is on *lockdown* status, meaning the occupants are confined to their rooms, officers pass the prisoners' meals through those door slots.

Also, when the prison is on lockdown, rules may require prisoners to be placed in handcuffs whenever they leave their cell. In lockdown situations, officers will order the prisoner to squat and maneuver his wrists through the slot in the door. The officer will fasten the man's hand in the steel cuffs, then direct the person to stand back while the guard unlocks the door. While on lockdown, people are handcuffed even as they walk to the shower. And in the penitentiary, it is not uncommon to be on lockdown for at least a few days each month, sometimes for weeks at a time.

Prisoners may purchase small Walkman-type radios or MP-3 players from the commissary, and they can listen through headphones. Radios with loudspeakers are not available or allowed. As a rule, federal prisoners do not have access to personal televisions, typewriters, or musical instruments. Rules limit the quantity of books a prisoner may keep in the cell. Generally, the rule is that a prisoner can keep five books in his possession at one time.

Like USPs, medium-security FCIs generally have two-man rooms. Well-behaved high-security prisoners may transfer from volatile USPs to less volatile FCIs. Quarters in virtually all of the medium-security FCIs resemble USP housing units.

Administrators in both the USPs and FCIs may have designated one of the housing units as an "honor dorm," which is considered preferred housing. If the prison has an honor dorm, individuals usually are assigned to that unit by application. The criteria for admission will include the prisoner's disciplinary record and seniority in the particular institution. Some of the perks associated with living in the honor dorm may include more access to the television rooms, or it simply may be a quieter environment. Silence and tranquility may be rare and cherished by some.

Low-security FCIs and Camps (FPCs):

Prisoners confined in low-security FCIs and camps, as a rule, have records that BOP administrators consider to be less threatening than the prisoners confined in medium- and high-security prisons. Generally, people in lower-security prison have fewer months remaining until release, and lower histories of documented violence.

Some people transfer to lower-security as a result of good behavior after many years in higher security. Disciplinary records influence custody ratings.

People can drop to lower security levels by participating in programs and avoiding disciplinary problems. Penitentiaries have no shortage of convicted murderers. If they serve 10 years without any infractions, their classification scoring will drop, thereby making them eligible for housing in a lower-security institution.

Low-security prisons, as a rule, require prisoners to have fewer than 20 years remaining to serve. Federal prison camps, as a rule, require prisoners to have fewer than 10 years remaining to serve. Besides the time remaining, prisoners in low and minimum-security prisons also must have the appropriate security scoring.

As a result of lower-security scores, operations in camps and low-security prisons are not as rigid the mediums and the highs. It costs taxpayers considerably more to operate medium- and high-security prisons. Administrators must assign more staff and manhours to operate them.

Lower-security institutions are less expensive to operate. Generally, prisoners in those facilities are not confined or locked in two-man rooms. Rather, they serve time in large dormitories or rooms holding many men. Although people in lower-security have a higher degree of freedom than the high- and medium-security prisoner, those in low and minimum-security sacrifice the relative privacy that comes with the two-man room.

This is not to imply that privacy (as the word is normally understood) is available in any prison. Readers should know that at any time, 24-hours a day, staff members have the right to open a door and order a prisoner to strip naked for a visual inspection.

At least a few times each year, officers will awaken people in the dead of night and order them to remove clothing. If a fight or violence breaks out, they may inspect all prisoners for marks or cuts. They investigate thoroughly, looking for leads that will help them determine which prisoners were involved.

» No person, in any prison setting, should have an expectation of privacy.

Some people prefer to serve sentences in higher security because of the two-man rooms. They know a staff member can open the door at any time, and that anyone can peer through the door's window. But for the most part, when the door in the room is closed, they are in their own shell and sharing it with only one other person.

Some people also like the fact that higher-security prisons have a single toilet and sink in the room, and only two people use it.

In low- and minimum-security prisons, on the other hand, prisoners use community bathrooms. When hundreds of men are sharing a bathroom facility, they sacrifice a degree of cleanliness.

As my partners Michael and Shon Hopwood have shown, people serving decades in any prison can be productive. Being productive requires a strong mindset, regardless of prison conditions.

In USPs and medium-security FCIs, prisoners are more likely to launch food strikes, work strikes, or riots. The herd mentality of the prison expects everyone to support the disturbance. In those facilities, men are exposed to more interference from others. That interference can hurt a person's plan to reach specific goals.

This is not to say that low-security facilities are without their share of problems. After all, perhaps hundreds of prisoners are confined inside these fences. Some of the people have 20 years remaining to serve and do not have hope for relief. An element of anger, hopelessness, depression, delusion, and despair exists in all prisons. Those combinations can be lethal anywhere, and it requires good critical-thinking skills to thrive.

Men sometimes learn that their families have deserted them. They may snap, act out aggressively over the most trivial matter. Still, as compared to higher-security institutions, the level of volatility is relatively lower in lows.

In camps, volatility rarely exists. In those institutions, people are much closer to their release dates. They're not looking to aggravate their problems by participating in the trivialities of prison living. That doesn't mean violence cannot erupt in a camp. But it's more episodic, not as frequent, and rarely as lethal.

As an example from a camp, one of my clients wrote a story that I'm cutting and pasting below:

My friend, Art, used to be a lawyer. Thinking he was doing a good deed, he got himself into some trouble. In an effort to protect food from being stolen from the kitchen, he reported the theft to guards.

Art paid a price.

First, people went into his cube and poured fish all over his clothes.

Then, they entered his cubicle a second time. They turned his locker upside down and emptied all contents of his locker, including food. They stole his radio and batteries.

I'm Art's friend and everybody knows it. Jay comes to my cube to walk after each meal. I never hesitate to be seen with him, even though I have been told he is considered a "rat".

These guys are making conscious decisions. They're being ostracized by the population. But they're not exposed to the type of retaliation that might exist in higher security prisons. People in prison should recognize that the culture is very different from the culture in society. Although every person must make his or, her own decision on how to adjust, it's important to remember that ramifications surrender every decision a person makes.

The dormitories of lower security prisons or camps may hold 100 people in a large room, the size of an aircraft hangar. Sometimes it's just long rows of bunk beds and lockers. In other facilities, the design breaks dormitories into two-man or four-man cubes, with the neck-high partitions that are familiar in office buildings. In addition to the bunk beds, the cubicles will have lockers, and perhaps a rod to hang clothes. They may have a small writing platform, too.

The environment of lower-security will be softer than in the penitentiary, and relatively more comfortable. Generally, each prisoner will be assigned his own chair. Instead of sleeping on thin mats, people may have an actual twin-size mattress. Again, people will be required to use community bathrooms, with long rows of toilets and sinks. In most cases, the toilets are partitioned off with the thin walls, like those in an airport bathroom. Showers, generally, will be in individual stalls; concerns over personal modesty should remain at home.

Initial Quarters Assignment:

The initial quarters assignment may be made at random, according to whichever bunk is available. Two completely incompatible prisoners may be assigned to share the same housing quarters. This presents more problems in the higher-security prisons than in the lower-security prisons. Some institutions authorize a unit officer to make bed changes. In most institutions, counselors must authorize the change.

With the First Step Act, people should be able to influence their quarters placement through participation in positive programs. As of this writing, in June of 2019, we have not seen how the BOP will interpret this provision of the First Step Act. We will write more in our course work on ResilientCourses.com as information becomes available to us.

If counselors assign a person to live with an incompatible cellmate, every day feels like a year.

In such situations, the prisoner has few options. He may try to resolve the matter by figuring out a truce with the cell mate. Otherwise, he may ask the unit manager to reassign him, or file a formal complaint through the administrative remedy procedure. Neither is a very attractive option, however, because the action will anger the counselor further. In most all situations, staff members support and respect each other's decisions. Some people choose to grovel, or whine, but that strategy rarely serves anyone's interest.

Options for Dealing with Incompatible Cellmates:

Within days after a counselor assigns a person to the general population, he will hear through the prisoner grapevine who is in charge of quarters assignments. Other prisoners also will be able to describe the staff member's policy on making bed moves.

If the word is out that the counselor is receptive to making changes, then all a person has to do is find someone with whom he is compatible, and then submit the copout ("Copout" *informal name that describes a request to staff*).

On the other hand, if the word is out that the Counselor has a policy of not making bed moves, then the prisoner is better off *not* requesting the change for a while. Instead, he may consider standing back to observe which people have influence with the difficult staff member.

Joseph's Story:

On Joseph's first day at a medium-security FCI, a guard led him to a two-man room. Joseph had begun his travels that morning before dawn. After several hours on government buses and planes, the staff processed him in. He felt tired. The lights were off in the room and the prisoner assigned to the lower bunk was lying on his bed.

"What do you want," the prisoner demanded when Joseph opened the door.

"I've been assigned here, top bunk."

The prisoner was silent. Joseph turned the light on.

"Turn off the light," came a bellow from the lower bunk. Joseph complied with the demand and he began feeling his way around the obscure room. It became obvious to Joseph that his new roommate was not interested in amicable relations.

There was no welcome, no greeting, no offer to provide him with toiletries or anything to help him settle in. There was not even an exchange of names. Instead, it was animosity from minute one. Not an easy way to begin serving time.

Over the next few days, hostilities in the room continued to escalate. Joseph walked on eggshells as he tiptoed around the small confines of the cell. He put himself at a disadvantage the moment he showed deference to his unknown cellmate. Surviving in prison may require immediate assertiveness. Ordering Joseph to turn off the light was a power move, and when Joseph complied, he gave off the impression that he could be controlled. Once he made that concession, the roommate—whose name was never offered—made it clear that Joseph was not welcome. Although authorities assigned Joseph to sleep there, the roommate was not going to make the living arrangements easy.

Since Joseph had a Counselor who would not make room changes, and because Joseph lacked the assertiveness to confront the hostility of his roommate, he responded by checking himself into protective custody (PC). Several weeks later he returned to the compound, but to a different room. By then he had been labeled as a weak inmate and he became the target of much more abuse within the prison.

Using the Influence of Others:

Counselors usually have many responsibilities. They are in charge of administering the visiting and phone lists of the prisoners who are on their caseload. They may be in charge of assigning jobs and monitoring the safety and sanitation requirements of the housing unit.

Counselors also have to take care of other trivial, clerical functions for the unit team. As a consequence, they frequently have one or two inmates to whom they feel comfortable delegating a portion of their work.

Some new people make it a point of observing and learning which prisoners have accrued such informal influence. When they do, they ask those prisoners to use their influence in persuading the counselor to make the requested change.

Prison rules strictly prohibit one inmate from giving anything of value to another inmate. That said, it's done daily. In later modules, and in our course lessons, we describe various prison hustles and the thriving underground economy that exists in every prison.

A prisoner that curries favor with a particular staff member frequently works as a lobbyist does outside. If a prisoner's objective is to be assigned to a particular bed, then he has to use critical-thinking skills.

He may have information that the staff member in charge of making bed changes is uncooperative. If that's the case, the prisoner may try using someone else's influence to help him accomplish his goal. Another prisoner may have influence and be able to help.

George's Story:

After leaving A&O, George, a new prisoner in his early 40s, was assigned to a 12-man room. The other 11 occupants were all in their 20s.

They played cards and dominoes on the room's table constantly. Since radios with speakers were not allowed, several of the room's occupants tuned their Walkman radios to the same hip-hop station. They blasted the music through headphones that they hung from their lockers.

There was never a moment's peace in the room. George knew he couldn't change the living patterns of the other 11 prisoners. He also knew that the counselor was uncooperative in making bed changes, especially for new inmates.

"I looked around. I saw this guy they called Mexico was real tight with the counselor," George explained. "Although he was a grouch with everyone else, the counselor seemed to rely on Mexico for all kinds of things. I went to Mexico with 10 cans of tuna and I asked him to help me move into a room that was quiet.

Since Mexico had been in the prison for a while, I figured he'd know the best room for me. I wanted to be around quiet guys. I didn't care where the room was, I just wanted some place I could sleep and read without people hollering all night.

If I got moved, I told Mexico that I'd give him 20 more cans of tuna. I don't know what he did and didn't ask how he did it. All I know is that the next day I was told to pack my belongings and move to my current bed. All's been well since the change."

Going Hard:

Other prisoners are indifferent to their bunk assignment. When they are assigned to a particular bed, they bring their belongings and "set up their house." They may not be looking for problems, but they certainly are not going to "punk out" as a hard prisoner would say that Joseph did. Nor would they consider going to a counselor or any other staff member for assistance. And there is no way in the world the hardened convict would ask another prisoner to assist him out of an uncomfortable situation. Rather, these prisoners act decisively, consequences be damned.

Texas Red's Story:

"I remember when I first rolled up into Lewisburg," Red described his stay. "We didn't have none of that A&O bullshit then. We was just dumped on the 'pound from the start. Know what I'm sayin'," he said. "Ain't no one up in the house when I come in, so I start unpackin' my shit," he explains.

"I'm standing on the chair as I'm makin' my rack, and this cocksucker moves up on in and starts with all this woo, woo, woo shit, tellin' me not to stand on his chair, not to move things around. 'Man, fuck all that bitch talk,' I told him. "I been put up in this motherfucker just like you. We're either gonna live together like men or you can get the fuck out.' I was lookin' at that motherfucker dead in his eyes, and he knew I was ready to take it to the wall if he came out the side of his neck wrong. He might of been strapped—I didn't give a fuck. I wasn't 'bout to listen to no bullshit in my house, know what I'm sayin' holm?"

Final Word:

A housing assignment can influence on an adjustment in prison. There is no place to be completely alone. Most all prisoners experience pockets of sadness, or even depression at certain times, when they realize that life outside is going on without them. There is also the constant humiliation of dealing with the rules and other prisoners. Life in prison can move along easier if a person can arrange an acceptable quarter's assignment.

As Mick Jagger sang, "You can't always get what you want. But if you try sometimes, you just might find, you get what you need."

Chapter 16

What Should I Know About Job Details?

Administrators assign prisoners to specific bunks. They also assign people to work on specific jobs. With few exceptions—like being in transit, in segregation, in an A&O program, or medically unassigned—all people in federal prison have job assignments, also known as work details.

Administrators assign prison jobs because they are convinced that excessive inmate idleness leads to disturbances within the prison.

Not all work details, or prison jobs, are equal. Some have the benefit of relatively high pay—less than $200 per month—but they come with the cost of more structure and responsibility.

Other jobs pay a prison "minimum wage," which amounts to less than $10 per month. Benefits with those jobs may be more free time.

Prison wages may seem absurdly low. As in all societies, labor is a supply and demand issue, and with an abundance of prisoners, wages are bound to be low.

Although staff members supervise and reign over every aspect of the prison, prison labor keeps it running. Prisoners unload all the food that comes into the warehouse. They work in the warehouses to store the food. They prepare and cook the food. Another work detail is responsible for cleaning the kitchen and the dining room where the prisoners eat.

Prison workers maintain the facilities, too. They work as electricians, as plumbers, and as carpenters. Some work in factory jobs, others teach classes.

Prisoners with administrative skills may work as clerks in any number of positions, or they may work in the education department as tutors. And hundreds of prisoners work on either landscaping crews or sanitation crews as orderlies.

There is no shortage of prison labor, but there is a shortage of prison jobs.

UNICOR Factory:

Many federal prisons operate factories that are part of the UNICOR corporation. UNICOR is a wholly owned government corporation, with annual sales in excess of $500-million. UNICOR uses prison labor to produce any number of products for government consumption. Some of the products UNICOR factories produce include mattresses, cables, military uniforms, mailbags for the postal services, sheets and towels for prisoners. Prison factories employ approximately 25 percent of the inmate labor force.

Generally, prisoners choose to work in prison factories because they have opportunities to earn higher pay—assuming they have a high school diploma or GED. Whereas most of the people in the general population work in jobs that pay less than 25-cents per hour, or an average of less than $20 per month, a long-tenured UNICOR worker that puts in overtime hours may earn in excess of $200 per month.

One of the catches for working in UNICOR, however, is that all UNICOR workers must agree to pay 50-percent of their income toward any financial obligation they received as a part of sentencing.

Many people love their UNICOR jobs. They enjoy the factory work because of the money they earn. Some also enjoy the challenges that come with doing something that they perceive as being meaningful.

Craig's Story:

"Even if they took away the pay, I'd still work in the UNICOR factory," Craig told members of our team. "I'm responsible for originating the paperwork and keeping track of all the shipping this factory does. I have a personal computer that is assigned to me, and I've been able to master many software programs. Even though I've been in prison for 10 years, I'm a whiz at working with complicated software programs. Because of my job I've picked up my typing speed to more than 100 words per minute. Most guys who have been in for 10 years don't have any skills. The skills I've developed will help me when I get out. Besides that, I like it in UNICOR. When I'm at work, I feel like I'm not even in prison. Besides that, I earn about two-hundred dollars every month."

Other prisoners aren't so impressed with the UNICOR operation. James described his experience.

James' Story:

"Man, fuck UNICOR. I worked there for two years. I went because I needed the money. I have a college degree and figured a factory job would give me a challenge. What a disappointment. First of all, I had to wait about four months before I could even get a job. And I was on the fast track waiting list because I have a fine.

My case manager made me sign some paper that said I agreed to give up half the wages I earned to pay for my fine. I was kind of pissed off about that, but I still thought it would be better than one of the other jobs. So I finally took a job in the payroll department.

"It's all automated," James continued. "The factory has a pretty sophisticated computer system that tracks all the labor and makes the appropriate journal entries to charge the expenses to the various jobs. The problem is that I work for these moron supervisors who can't spell *cat*. They relied on me to do everything, and I didn't even mind it. What really pissed me off about the whole thing was that although they expected me to work for them, if I was late coming back from lunch because a gate was locked, or if I wanted to participate in a class or something, the staff member would always give me hell—like I was asking for some kind of favor.

They spend their time yacking on the phone all day, but they expect us worker bees to do everything. It wouldn't be so bad if they didn't treat us like shit. Since they were takin' half my pay anyway, I quit."

Besides providing employment to the inmate population, the profits that UNICOR generates are plied back into the prison to fund educational and recreational programs. Although James didn't like it, UNICOR played a significant role on almost every federal prison compound. It provides a payroll that may exceed $50,000 per month. That money goes directly into the inmate accounts. The inmates use that money to pay their fines, to purchase items from the commissary, to support their family members, to fuel the underground economy, and to save for their release.

Commissary Jobs:

Those who work in the prison commissary are also high earners. Under staff supervision, commissary workers are responsible for unloading, stacking, and keeping an inventory of all the items sold in the inmate store. The commissary is not like a grocery store, where prisoners browse through the lines with a cart and choose what they want. Instead, each prisoner is given a menu of items that are available in the commissary.

The prisoner marks the quantity of items he wants on the list and passes the list through a bank teller-like window to a staff member. The staff member then gives the list to a commissary worker. The worker serves as a kind of runner, gathering all the items on the list and placing them in a basket. The staff member then rings the list up and charges the inmate's account.

Although they are among the highest-paid jobs in the prison, commissary workers also are among the hardest working. Other jobs, including UNICOR, are overstaffed. Perhaps ten people in other prison jobs would be assigned to a duty that one person in the community would complete. Not so for commissary workers. Because staff members in the commissary do not have the room to featherbed their department with idle workers, those who work in the commissary are required to work rather hard throughout their shift. It's a demanding job.

"I like working in the commissary for a few reasons," Bob explained. "One is that I get paid well. Another is that I'm allowed to shop whenever I want." Generally, prisoners are only allowed to shop in the commissary once or twice each week on specified days. Because Bob works in the commissary, he shops whenever he is on duty as a perquisite of the job. "I also like it because the busy schedule helps my time pass," Bob added. He earns close to $200 per month.

Food Service:

There are scores of jobs available in the Food Service Department, which employs approximately 15 percent of the prison's population.

The highest paid jobs in Food Services usually go to those prisoners who work in the warehouse and the clerks who fill out the payroll forms. Those workers earn approximately $100 per month.

Cooks are more or less the next level, and they earn somewhere between $80 and $100 per month. The rest of the workers usually earn anywhere from $20 to $70 per month, and may have jobs washing dishes, pots and pans, or performing cleaning services.

Some people enjoy working in Food Services because they eat well. The job may also provide a means of supplementing income by stealing food from the kitchen to sell in the housing units.

Prisoners that steal accept a high risk. If staff members catch anyone stealing, they may charge the person with a high-severity disciplinary infraction. An active kitchen thief in a large prison may supplement his income by several hundred dollars each month.

Prisoners who do not want to steal complain of Food Services as being one of the least-desirable details. It's a tough place to work because it's busy. Perhaps 90 percent of the prisoner population eats in the chow hall every day, making it a high-stress area of the prison. It's also noisy. Staff members try to speed through meal times, making the job feel demanding for some, with relatively little pay.

Central Maintenance Services (CMS):

This department includes the electric shop, plumbing shop, carpentry shop, paint shop, and other mechanical services. People assigned to these jobs maintain the prison's facilities. Most prisons have apprenticeship programs for people that want to develop skills as craftsmen in these trades. When they are on the job, CMS workers earn anywhere between $20 and $80 per month, depending on the seniority of the worker—not on how much one knows, and not necessarily on how hard one works.

Education Jobs:

The Education Department offers many jobs, including librarians, tutors, and clerks. Many inmates prefer these jobs because the Education Department gives them an opportunity to pass their time in a relatively quiet environment. Some derive a sense of meaning by helping others, or learning. Jobs in Education pay relatively poorly. Most workers earn fewer than $20 per month since education is not a high priority of the institution.

Our partner Shon used his time as a law library clerk in an extremely effective way. Those who've read his book, *Law Man* know the full story. While in prison, he became skilled in understanding the law.

Shon's skill led to his helping many people. Some got time cuts and left prison early. He wrote motions that led to changes in the law. And upon his release, the Bill and Melinda Gates Foundation gave him a scholarship to the University of Washington Law School. He became a clerk for federal judges, and then a professor at Georgetown Law School.

Shon is an inspiration to anyone. He shows that regardless of what bad decisions a person has made in the past, it's never too late to start sowing seeds for a better future. He prepared himself for success while serving time inside of a medium-security prison, alongside others that wasted time.

Andrew's Story:

"My first job here was as a tutor in education," Andrew told members of our team. "I hold a master's degree in Romance Languages, and since I had to serve time in prison, I figured I'd get back into teaching. They called me a tutor, but no staff member ever did more than take roll in the classroom. I taught English as a Second Language and the Spanish GED program. The job required me to be there for seven hours each day and I wasn't too crazy about that.

I earned $14 per month for my work, and the guys really liked the way I taught. I got ticked off when I heard that the guy who was cleaning the bathrooms—who only had to be there for about two hours each day—was making $17 per month. When I heard about the discrepancy in pay, I realized how little the staff appreciated my work.

It wasn't really the money. Who really cares about three bucks? I just felt as if I were an idiot being there. Wanting a change, I sought a job as a unit orderly. I clean my little area and after that I'm free to do what I want. It takes me no more than an hour each day. I make more now than I did when I was responsible for teaching 100 students. I still help the other people, but I do it on my own time."

Do-nothing Jobs:

When Andrew switched from the Education Department to a job as a unit orderly, he was switching to a do-nothing job. With the prison system so crowded, there are more prisoners than jobs available. As a result, people that have been in the prison for a long time hold on to the good jobs. There may be long waiting lists to move into high-paying or good positions.

Prisoners may define a "good" position differently. Andrew enjoyed having his time free, so he wanted a job where he would be left alone after completing his duties. As a unit orderly, Andrew had to sweep a staircase a few times each day. Other than that, he was free to stay in his housing unit working on his own projects.

Bob, who worked in the commissary, would not have considered such a job ideal. Bob enjoyed the structure of keeping busy. He said the job made his time pass easier. He also appreciated the higher earnings. Craig enjoyed the responsibilities that came with his UNICOR position. Each prisoner can work to maneuver his way into a good job, but he may have to wait in line for another prisoner to leave before the right job opens.

Working One's Way into the Right Job:

Within days after the prisoner clears the A&O process, a counselor will assign him to a job if he has not already found one. That's why one of the *first* things a person ought to do after he arrives at a prison is to locate a job that suits him. Some jobs are easy to get into, others take a while.

UNICOR jobs have a long waiting list. Staff members generally control those waiting lists. If the prisoner has special skills that the factory needs (there always is a need for competent clerks), they may avoid the waiting list. Otherwise, individuals who want to work in UNICOR will be placed on one of three waiting lists.

- » The first list is a UNICOR-prior list, and only inmates who worked in UNICOR at their prior institution will be placed on that list.
- » The second list is the FRP-wait list, which is for those inmates who owe at least $1,000 as part of their criminal sentence. Administrators give those inmates priority in UNICOR jobs because half the prisoner's monthly pay will go toward the financial obligation related to the criminal sentence.
- » Prisoners who want to work in UNICOR but do not fit into one of the other two categories will be placed on the general-UNICOR waiting list. It may take three years for those prisoners to be assigned to the factory.

In most jobs besides those in the factory, certain prisoners have a high degree of influence in shaping the work-detail roster. Either they manage the rosters themselves, or they work closely with a staff supervisor who assigns the prison job. It is important for newly arriving inmates to figure out what it is they want to do with their time. If they have the requisite skills and want structure and quiet in their day, they may pursue a job in education. If they want freedom, they may look for a job as a unit orderly.

Whatever they choose, they ought to get information from others in the population. Ordinarily, there will be a few prisoners with influence. New prisoners may benefit from finding those people with influence. Listen, learn, and work toward finding a job that will ease the adjustment inside.

Gordon's Story:

"I began looking for a job as soon as I cleared A&O. I didn't know anyone in the prison. I had 20 months to serve, and all I knew was that I didn't want to work in Food Service. I enjoy reading, so I tried to get a job in the library. Since I was new, I didn't know any prisoners.

I went to the staff member who ran the library and asked her to sign a copout so I could work for her. She accepted my copout and said she would take care of it. Then, a week later, I saw my name on the callout sheet. I got assigned to work in Food Services, just what I didn't want. Worse still, because I was a new prisoner, they were posting me to the least desirable shift—I was going to work scrubbing pots and pans.

Later, Gordon found another prisoner that had some influence. Gordon said he gave him $25 worth of commissary after he got hired to become a librarian.

Camp Drivers:

In minimum-security camp, some people are assigned as "drivers." They leave the camp every day in a car. They drive to local stores or businesses to run errands for staff members.

When Michael was confined at the Lompoc Camp, he told me about a person that had an unusual job as a long-distance truck driver.

The camp in Lompoc operated a dairy. The dairy, with several hundred head of cattle, produced milk. People in the prison processed the milk into containers.

The inmate driver transported the milk to other federal prisons. He left the prison each week and spent days on the road, driving the truck from California to Arizona and back. While traveling, the driver slept in a roadside motel and he ate in restaurants. The inmate driver may have been serving time, but he was on the road several days each week without any supervision.

Michael said there were only two or three "camp driver" positions. And they rarely became available. Many staff members were involved in the decision of which person to hire for the role.

Chapter 17

What Should I know About
Education and Recreation in Prison?

Some people want to use their time in prison productively. By participating in educational programs, people can develop skills and credentials that translate into success. Those programs may be informal, without any type of certificate or credential.

As described earlier, our partner Shon taught himself how to research the law and how to file motions in court. There wasn't any formal program to teach people legal research, but he learned on his own.

Similarly, when Michael began serving his sentence, he reached out to connect with universities. Despite not have any financial resources, by writing, he opened opportunities that led to a bachelor's degree and a master's degree. Then, he leveraged those credentials to lead a productive life through the decades he served.

As he described in *Earning Freedom,* he build a publishing career and launched other ventures from inside prison boundaries.

While serving my sentence, I worked closely with Michael to author books and sow seeds that would lead to several successful businesses after I got out.

When there is a will there is a way. We recommend that people use their time wisely while in prison. A good use of time helps a person recalibrate, making all the difference in the world.

We've seen literature indicating that only 37 percent of the prison population participates in prison education. That figure is misleading. It's misleading because it only measure inmates participating in programs sponsored by the system.

The statistic doesn't measure progress of people that study independently. For example, neither Shon's independent study that prepared him for law school, nor Michael's independent study that led to graduate degrees and a publishing career, nor my work to become a writer, teacher, and communicator would be reflected in government statistics.

We studied independently, and we made progress.

Still, in light of the First Step Act, every person in prison should learn more about the educational system in prison. Learning how to work through it can lead to "Earned Time" credits, which can translate into an earlier transition to home confinement.

Each federal prison has an Education Department staffed by a Supervisor of Education (SOE) and several teachers. The Department is mandated to provide courses in basic literacy (ABE), classes that lead toward obtaining a high school equivalency diploma (GED), and classes in English as a second language (ESL).

Besides those basic courses, every federal prison offers a variety of vocational programs (VT). Some of the more popular VT programs include courses in picture framing, woodworking, culinary arts, electronics, and basic computer software applications.

Finally, skillful prisoners may write a curriculum of their own and teach Adult Continuing Education (ACE) courses.

People lead courses or workshops on writing, understanding the stock market, foreign language, small business management, and other topics.

With passage of the First Step Act, funding is supposed to be freed up to offer additional educational and vocational programming. We'll report on that information in our course as the policies become available.

We anticipate that more community colleges or universities will offer coursework for people in prison. Some prisons already have relationships with colleges, but that is an institution-by-institution arrangement. When policies become systemic, we will report on what we learn at ResilientCourses.com.

Adult Basic Education Courses (ABE):

Many people may not know how to read or write when they start serving the sentence. The ABE courses are remedial in nature, helping get people ready for the GED program.

People that cannot verify educational credentials are required to take a simple test to measure their level of literacy. Administrators require those that do not score above the eighth-grade level to enroll in ABE courses. If they refuse to participate, staff may take disciplinary action or withhold privileges.

High School Equivalency Course (GED):

Those functioning above the eighth-grade level, but don't have a verified high school diploma or its equivalency are required to participate in the GED program. People who have a high school diploma or its equivalency ought to provide proof to the probation officer during the pre-sentence investigation.

If the PSR says, "defendant indicates he graduated high school," BOP staff members may not consider that information sufficient to waive the GED-program requirement.

The PSR must say that the probation officer *verified* that the offender has the required credentials in order to be exempt from the GED program. People in prison should be aware that some BOP officials will not accept a college degree as a substitute for the high school diploma. Staff members can be sticklers for policy.

People that cannot verify they attained high school equivalency are prohibited from earning higher than a grade-four on the inmate pay scale. Essentially, that means the person is limited to earning less $20 per month, regardless of which job he performs or how well he performs it. If a person doesn't have a GED, or at least participate in programs that lead to the GED, the prisoner may lose access to good time, too.

Again, the First Step Act incentivizes people to participate in educational programs. Our team believes that participating in educational programs—whether independently or through structured courses—is an outstanding way to prepare for success.

English as a Second Language Course (ESL):

A BOP publication indicates that 31.6 percent of the population is of Hispanic origin, and 30 percent are foreign nationals. The BOP offers courses to help those people learn how to speak English.

Vocational Training Programs (VT):

All federal prisons offer a few VT programs. They have structured curriculums mixed with classroom instruction, as well as "live-work" projects. For example, in the wood-working program prisoners participate in several weeks of classroom and shop instruction. Then, those who develop skills build cabinets for various offices around the institution. They may repair desks or install bookshelves. All of the VT programs result in certificates. Some of the VT programs are extensive, requiring as many as 8,000 hours to complete. The successful participants may earn accredited journeyman's certificates.

As with jobs, there may be long waiting lists to participate in VT programs. The BOP offers people an opportunity to transfer on a temporary basis to institutions where specific VT programs may be available. After the individual completes the program, he usually will return to his institution of origin.

Andre's Story:

"I started serving a 17-year sentence in 1992," Andre told members of our team. "I quit high school when I was in the 11th grade, so I enrolled in the GED program right away when I got to prison. Then, in 1993 I enrolled in the college program and I did really well. But the funding for four-year college programs stopped in 1994 so I couldn't continue.

I heard about a job in UNICOR where guys could learn something about computer drafting, so I applied for the job. One day when I was in Education I asked the teacher to let me look through one of the books that listed the educational courses available in other prisons. I found a two-year VT program in computer drafting at a Texas prison, so I requested an educational transfer. I went out there and completed the program.

I got an AA degree from a community college out there, and a certificate in computer drafting. They transferred me back to New Jersey after I finished the program," Andre said. "Now I'm hoping to find another program to carry me through a couple more years."

Adult Continuing Education Courses (ACE):

Some of the men in each prison have advanced skills and they create courses to teach others. The system allows ACE instructors to teach on a volunteer basis. Teaching an ACE course does not excuse the instructor from his obligation to hold a prison job.

College Studies:

As mentioned earlier, some prisons have contractual relationships with community colleges that allow people to earn two-year degrees.

If a prisoner has access to outside funding, four-year degrees may be available through independent study. People that want to pursue such programs will need to be relentless in their self-advocacy.

Several accredited universities offer correspondence programs. It takes persistence and commitment, but it's worth the effort. Michael wrote that while he was working toward university degrees, he felt more like a student than a prisoner. Studying toward a meaningful goal is an excellent pathway to building a strong mindset.

Leisure Library:

The Education Department also oversees the leisure library. Some libraries stock well over 10,000 books, but others have paltry libraries. The libraries grow from donations. People donate books they receive from family. Besides books on the library shelves, most libraries participate in the inter-library lending program. Through that program, a person can request books that may not be available on the bookshelves.

Besides offering books, libraries may also subscribe to newspapers and magazines. Sometimes they make courses available. Reading and learning provides a mental escape to the monotony of prison. And with the First Step Act, documenting progress can lead to additional privileges.

Law Library:

Besides the leisure library, each federal prison offers a relatively extensive law library. It offers the *Federal Supplement*, *Federal Reporter*, and *Lawyer's Edition* series of books through a digital platform.

People can learn from published decisions from the district courts, appellate courts, and Supreme Court. It also offers the *Shepherd's Citation* series and other supplemental reading to help individuals keep abreast of changes in the law. It's difficult for people to litigate from inside the fences. Yet with the law library, it's not impossible, as our partner Shon showed.

Recreational Programs:

Prisons offer a variety of indoor and outdoor recreational facilities. Depending on security levels, it's like a high school track-and-field area, with a lot of fences and without members of the opposite gender. Older prisons offer extensive weight-training facilities. Newer prisons may not have weights, but they may have strength-training machines. Some gymnasiums offer aerobic machines and racquetball or handball courts. They also have game rooms with pool tables and card games.

Prisons have softball fields, soccer fields, and volleyball courts. There's also a running track and basketball courts.

The prisons organize teams, usually according to housing units, that participate in seasonal sports. The best players come together to form varsity teams and staff from the Recreation Department may coordinate with community groups to organize teams from outside to come and play against the people inside.

The Recreation Department has a role inside the housing units, too. Each housing unit has several televisions, usually wall mounted. The audio is broadcast on FM frequencies and people listen to television through their Walkman radios.

Hobby-craft Programs:

Besides sports, the Recreation Department also sponsors several hobby craft programs. Depending on the prison, courses in leather craft, acrylic and oil painting, drawing, pottery, ceramics, and other programs may be available. In crowded prisons, programs may have extensive waiting lists.

Administrators sometimes limit the quantity of time individuals can spend in them. Ordinarily, rules require people to send their completed hobby craft projects home.

As people pass years away from their communities, family, and loved ones, they need activities to keep their minds and bodies active. Education and recreation programs help reduce some of the tension that inevitably comes with confinement. They also provide opportunities for people to enrich their lives, developing skills that will remain with them even after confinement ends.

Prisoners may enter the system in poor physical condition and with substandard education levels. With discipline, they can develop routines that lessen stress and improve their quality of life. Growing in an environment marked by adversity builds character and self-esteem.

Chapter 18

What Should I Know About RDAP and Psychology Programs?

Being separated from family, anxieties about the future, and other complications of prison life can lead to depression, or even more severe mental health problems. For that reason, every federal prison offers a Psychology Department with at least one psychologist on staff. They offer a combination of group programs. In some cases, the Psychology Department may offer individual counseling sessions.

Most of the attention in the Psychology Department goes to the substance-treatment programs. According to BOP literature, approximately 40 percent of the people in prison have histories of drug abuse. In 1996, the U.S. Congress began appropriating millions of dollars to fund drug treatment programs in federal prison.

There are at least three separate psychology programs designed to help people resolve substance-abuse problems.

The first program takes place over a few weeks, lasting between 12 to 15 hours. People going through that simple program receive literature, watch videos, and listen to discussions about the ways that drug abuse interferes with possibilities of successful living.

A second program spans over several months. Staff from the psychology department meet with people enrolled in the group class for about two hours at a time. They watch videos, work through a curriculum, write essays, and discuss the various ways that substance abuse has led to problems. This treatment program, known as the Non-Residential Drug Abuse Program, is available to anyone that wants to enroll. Psychologists consider it a stepping stone to the most popular program, known as the Residential Drug Abuse Program (RDAP).

Residential Drug Abuse Program (RDAP):

The RDAP program is popular with people in prison because it can result a time cut. It is identified as a "residential" program because it reserves a specific housing unit for each person assigned to the program. Since RDAP is not available in every federal prison, people may sometimes start serving their terms in one prison, but then transfer to a prison that offers RDAP when they closer to their release date.

The RDAP program is also known as the 500-hour drug treatment program. People that participate in RDAP spend about four hours together each day in a group session or on independent study projects. Staff from the Psychology Department teach programs based on cognitive behavioral therapy. Basically, those programs endeavor to influence more positive living and thinking habits. Through a series of courses that include open-ended questions, essays, videos, reading, lectures, and personal accountability metrics, RDAP teaches lessons on the power of introspection.

Anyone may volunteer to participate in RDAP, but not everyone will be accepted. And in order to receive the time cut, a person must qualify.

How to Qualify for RDAP:

The psychology department at each prison will

have a process to consider applications that people may submit if they want to participate in RDAP. After a person submits a request to participate in RDAP, a series of interviews will begin. To qualify:

» The person should have more than 24 months to serve on the sentence.

» The person should be able to document that he has a history of substance abuse during the 12-month period that preceded the arrest for the current offense.

» The person should not have any serious mental problems.

» The person must know how to read and write in order to complete the program.

» The person should not have any issues that could result in deportation.

» The person should not have any history of violence or weapons.

In practice, the Presentence Investigation Report will be the most relevant documentation when it comes to qualifying for the RDAP program.

The more evidence a person can provide to show a history of substance abuse, the better. But in practice, to qualify easily, a person should admit to substance abuse within the 12 months that preceded the arrest. If the person makes such an admission during the interview with the probation officer for the presentence investigation report, that self-reporting may suffice. The more verification, the better.

Program Statement 5330.11 provides some guidance on what psychology staff must consider for RDAP applicants. The staff is supposed to review the

PSR to assess whether the applicant meets the diagnostic criteria for abuse or dependence on the *Diagnostic and Statistical manual of Mental Disorders, Fifth Edition (DSM-V).*

The substance abuse doesn't have to be linked to the offense, and a judge doesn't have to recommend RDAP.

Unfortunately, many people do not want to reveal their problems with substance abuse when they meet with a probation officer. They believe that discussing substance abuse may result in an unfavorable assessment of the person.

People that minimize their experience with substance abuse may face challenges in being accepted into the RDAP program. The higher the level of documentation they can provide, the more they strengthen their application. If a person tells a probation officer that he used drugs or drinks recreationally, or socially, the report may not help. Staff members may obstruct their efforts to qualify for RDAP.

Defendants that want to qualify for RDAP should discuss their interest with the defense attorney or with someone else that has knowledge of RDAP.

Members on our team have extensive knowledge of RDAP, and they can provide personal guidance. If the person failed to reveal everything to the probation officer, then it may be important to gather other evidence to verify substance abuse.

It would also be helpful for the attorney to make a solid case for the defendant to become a candidate for RDAP during the sentencing hearing. He may ask the judge to recommend RDAP in the "Statement of Reasons."

The judge should make a finding that states the defendant had a substance-abuse problem during the past 12 months and that he wants the defendant to get treatment while in prison.

Other documentation that help a person overcome insufficient PSR documentation include:

» Documentation from a substance abuse treatment provider.

» Documentation from a licensed healthcare professional that diagnosed and treated the person during the 12-month period before the person's arrest on the instant offense.

» Proof of two or more convictions for driving while intoxicated within the five years before the arrest.

Some categories of offenses or conviction-status make people *ineligible* for the time cut from RDAP. They may include:

» Immigration and Customs Enforcement detainees

» Inmates that have not yet been convicted of a crime

» People that were not convicted in federal court

» Inmates with detainers that preclude halfway house placement

» Inmates with a history of violent offenses

Stated reasons for ineligibility for early release from RDAP include prior felony or misdemeanor conviction for any of the following offenses:

- Homicide
- Forcible rape
- Robbery
- Aggravated assault
- Arson
- Kidnapping,
- Sexual abuse upon minors

Current felony conviction for an element that includes attempted force against a person or property

- An offense that involves the carrying, possession, or use of a firearm or other dangerous weapon
- An offense that includes a serious potential risk of physical force, or
- An offense that involves sexual abuse against minors
- People that got the benefit of RDAP on a previous conviction

Amount of Reduction:

Not everyone qualifies for the maximum of 12-month sentence reduction. The amount of time off depends upon the length of sentence imposed:

» Sentence of 37 months or longer: Receive up to 12 months off the sentence upon the completion of the program.

» Sentence of between 31 and 36 months: Receive up to nine months off the sentence upon the completion of the program.

» Sentence of less than 30 months: Receive up to six months off the sentence.

In addition to the time cut, people that complete RDAP will also receive at least six months of placement in community confinement. With the First Step Act, they may get to serve the final year of their sentence in a community confinement center (halfway house / home confinement).

The Psychology Department offers other programs at specific institutions. As of this writing, those programs do not result in any type of time cut. Those other psychology programs include:

Bureau Rehabilitation and Values Enhancement (BRAVE) Program:

This program is only offered at FCI Beckley medium and FCI Victorville medium. It is designed for people that are 32 years of age or younger, and they have 60 months or longer to serve. Completion of BRAVE may spare those people being transferred to a USP. It focuses on helping people develop interpersonal skills and improving their attitude so they don't get into more problems in prison.

Challenge Program:

This is a program for people in some high-security prisons. Participants must have a history of substance abuse or major mental illness like psychotic disorder, mood disorders, anxiety disorders, or personality disorders. It's a residential program in penitentiaries and may help people avoid some of the volatility of high security. It's currently available at:

» Big Sandy, KY

» Hazelton, WV

- Lee, VA
- McCreary, KY
- Terre Haute, IN
- Allenwood, PA
- Canaan, PA
- Beaumont, TX
- Coleman, FL
- Pollock, LA
- Tucson, AZ
- Atwater, CA

Resolve Program:

The Resolve Program is mostly reserved for female inmates that have histories of trauma. Program participants learn to cope with the trauma, using curriculum, videos, counseling, and other cognitive processing therapy. It's available in the following prisons:

- Alderson, WV
- Hazelton WV
- Lexington, KY
- Greenville, IL
- Waseca, MN
- Danbury, CT
- Florence, CO
- Bryan, TX
- Carswell, TX

- Aliceville, AL
- Coleman, FL
- Marianna, FL
- Tallahassee, FL
- Dublin, CA
- Victorville, CA

Sex Offender Treatment Program (Non-Residential)

Most participants in the SOTP-NR have a history of a single sex crime. They are usully first-time offenders serving a sentence for an Internet sex offense. The program is voluntary, and available at the following prisons:

- Petersburg, VA
- Englewood, CO
- Marion, IL
- Elkton, OH
- Carswell, TX
- Seagoville, TX
- Mariana, FL
- Tucson, AZ

Sex Offender Treatment Program (Residential)

Participants in the SOTP-R have a history of multiple sex crimes, extensive non-sexual criminal histories, and or a high level of sexual deviancy or hypersexuality. The progam is voluntary. Prior to placement in the the program, the must be screened and accepted.

» Marion, IL

» FMC Devens, MA

Skills Program:

This program is for male inmates with significant functional impairment due to intellectual disabilities, neurological deficits, and social skills deficits. They must be eligible for housing in low or medium security. They must volunteer, have no history of sexual predatory violence, and be within 24 months of release when they begin the program.

» Danbury, CT

» Coleman, FL

Steps Toward Emotional Growth and Awareness Program (STAGES)

Inmates referred to the STAGES Program have a primary diagnosis of Borderline Personality Disorder and a history of unfavorable institutional adjustment linked to this disorder.

Examples of unfavorable institutional adjustment include multiple incident reports, suicide watches, and/or extended placement in restrictive housing. Inmates designated to the STAGES Program must volunteer for treatment and be willing to actively engage in the treatment process. Willingness to engage in the treatment is assessed through a brief course of pre-treatment in which the inmate learns basic skills at the referring institution.

» Terre Haute, IN

- Florence, CO

Life Connections Program (LCP)

The LCP is a residential faith-based program offered to inmates of all faith traditions, including for those who do not hold to a religious preference. This program is available to offenders at low, medium, and high security facilities. The goal of LCP is to provide opportunities for the development and maturation of the participants' commitment to normative values and responsibilities, resulting in overall changed behavior and better institutional adjustments. In addition, the participants receive life skills and practical tools and strategies to assist them in transitioning back to society once released from federal custody.

Program admission criteria are as follows:

- Low and medium security male offenders within 24 to 36 months of their projected release date.
- High security male offenders with 30 months or more prior to their projected release date.
- Low security female offenders with 30 months or more prior to their projected release date.
- Must not have a written deportation order.
- Must not be on Financial Responsibility Program (FRP) Refuse status.
- Must have met English as a Second Langue (ESL) and GED obligations.
- Must receive recommendation

Available:

- Petersburg, VA
- Leavenworth, KS

- Milan, MI
- Terre Haute, IN
- Carswell, TX

Chapter 19

What Religious Services are Available?

Religious services help many people cope with the challenges of confinement. To support religious programs, the Bureau of Prisons employs more than 200 chaplains. Besides the chaplains, approximately 10,000 volunteers and contractors support the religious programs. Ample opportunities exist for people in prison to worship and practice their religious faith.

Like all BOP employees, the chaplain "is a correctional officer first." Keep this fact in mind during worshipping practices, because it's not unusual for chaplains or rabbis to write disciplinary infractions. People should not expect confidentiality when talking with any staff member, or for that matter, with anyone else in prison.

Chaplains may be of any religious group, and it's not unusual for a them to interact with people of different faiths. Christian chaplains, Jewish rabbis, and Islamic imams may lead worshipping services for any group.

The First Amendment of the U.S. Constitution guarantees all Americans the right to practice their religious beliefs. Prisons have limits, however. The BOP does not condone all worship practices. Some Native American religions, for example, worship using the "peace pipe" and peyote in their services.

To be consistent with its commitment to policy, the BOP identified 31 different religious groups that it has authorized. Individuals who want to come together and worship must identify their religion as belonging to one of those groups the BOP recognizes. Regardless of group, all people in the prison can use the multi-faith chapel.

The Multi-faith Chapel:

That main chapel serves as an assembly room for other non-religious programs that require seating for several hundred people. Additionally, the chapel building usually has several smaller rooms for religious groups that meet in smaller numbers.

Besides using the chapel for prayer, many prisoners go to the chapel in search of silence. Chapels, like the education department, can be a respite inside the confines of a prison.

Chapels may also include a library that includes a variety of books that may be of interest to individuals of particular faiths. Some of those books are for reference only, and inmates are not permitted to remove them. Reading in the chapel is not a problem, though, as it usually has the most comfortable seating in the prison.

Chapels may have music room with a piano and an organ along with many other instruments. Groups meet to practice in the music room, and regularly perform during the religious services. The chapels also sponsor an audio-visual program, where video and audiocassettes of a religious nature are available.

Byron's Story:

Byron told members of our team that authorities arrested him when he was 19 for charges related to the distribution of cocaine. He received a 20-year sentence and felt like he was coping well, largely because of religious services. Prison didn't bother him at all, he said.

Byron came from a large urban housing project and was no stranger to violence. He had been gang affiliated as a young man. When he started serving his sentence, however, he picked up a Bible. Although not religious prior to confinement, faith changed his life.

"I used to worry about my time. But once I picked up the Bible, it changed my whole outlook," Byron explained. "I've been reading it ever since. Whenever I'm not working on my job, or exercising, I go to the chapel and participate in one of the programs. I'm there every day. On Sundays, I'm active in the Christian services. On other days, I'm either involved with a prayer group, a Bible-study group, or singing with the choir. Because of services in the Chapel, I don't even feel as if I'm in prison. Ten years have passed since my arrest. For me, not one day has been wasted. I feel as though this is where God wants me to be. I've learned to put everything in God's hands."

Native Americans:

Besides the regular Chapel, each federal prison provides an area for Native Americans who practice their spirituality in ways that are distinct from other organized religious groups.

To show how the BOP makes an extra effort to accommodate all religious groups, we'll provide detail of what the system makes available for Native Americans at some prisons where members of our team have been held.

Services for the Native Americans take place entirely outside, climate notwithstanding. Unlike most of the other programs sponsored by the chapel, the Native Americans make little use of a chaplain—prisoners and volunteers from the community basically conduct the services.

Generally, the area where Native Americans worship is immediately outside the chapel building, or near the recreation yard. They have a small fenced-in area, about 500 square-feet. Native Americans who participate in the program meet in the outside area on Friday evenings to participate in what they call "The Talking Circle." Those who pass through The Talking Circle ritual are eligible to sweat on Saturday, when the sweat lodge is put into use. Again, staff members need not be present for this gathering.

When not in use, the sweat lodge looks like a wooden, dome-shaped frame. It's made of natural tree branches, about 10-feet in diameter, and less than 6-feet high. The lodge has a bare earth floor. Directly in the center, there is a pit about 30-inches in diameter and 12-inches deep. This is where the prisoners put the red-hot rocks (some people refer to the rocks as "the grandfathers") when the sweat lodge is in use.

Early on Saturday mornings, people responsible for coordinating the sweat build a roaring bonfire outside of the sweat lodge with logs provided by the chaplain. When it's hot enough, they place rocks in the fire. While the fire is being built, other people cover the sweat lodge frame with canvas tarps.

On top of the tarps, they place many layers of wool blankets. When it's finished, the lodge looks like a covered dome with a small opening. Guards would not be able to monitor what is going on inside the covered dome without entering, and it's nearly pitch-black inside.

When the rocks are red hot, one prisoner will dig them out of the fire with a shovel—one rock at a time. He'll carry the rock to the flap in the dome. By then, several Native Americans will be inside the dome. They usually have stripped down to a pair of shorts and sit on a blanket they place upon the ground. One of the people inside the dome will retrieve the rock from the shovel and place it in the dome's pit; he uses a pair of animal antlers as tongs to grab and carry the red-hot rock. As the rock is being placed in the pit, all of the prisoners inside the dome yell, "Welcome grandfather."

There is a method to the quantity of rocks that are brought into the dome. Once the appropriate number of red-hot rocks are inside, the flap of the dome is closed. Native Americans chant ritual songs appropriate to their service—and they sweat. It gets very hot inside the dome. Those participating say that they feel cleansed and elevated through the process.

Other religious groups get similar worshipping programs that are unique to their faith. For example, people that practice the Jewish faith get to practice Shabbat services on specific evenings; people that practice Islam get accommodations for the Ramadan season.

Chapter 20

What if I need Medical Attention in Prison?

All prisons employ teams of medical staff for people in need of healthcare. They include at least one physician, nurse practitioners or physician assistants, nurses, dentists, hygienists, and technicians. Like anywhere else in society, some people are in need of more healthcare services than others. Authorities designate people with chronic healthcare needs to prisons that operate as medical centers.

In an effort to minimize malingering and the wasteful use of medical resources, policies require people to make payments if they ask to see someone from healthcare. At less than $10 per visit, those costs seem negligible by society's standards. To put those costs in perspective, remember that some prison jobs result in less than $10 per month in earnings. If a person doesn't keep money in the account, he may not have to pay for healthcare costs.

Each prison will have its own policy for how to access healthcare procedures. What follows is a summary of what to expect—broadly speaking. These are descriptions from a typical prison, rather than from a designated federal medical center. We also offer commentary from people in prison that we've interviewed.

We offer insight into four different aspects of medical treatment:

» sick call,

» emergency medical problems,

» illnesses requiring regular monitoring, and

» special surgery.

Sick Call:

The term "sick call" refers to the initiation of medical treatment. Either a staff member or a person in prison may start the sick call process. In other words, staff members may want to call upon a person for a routine examination. The staff member may put the person on sick call. Likewise, a person may not feel well and want to see a doctor or a nurse. The prisoner would submit a request to go to sick call.

Except in emergencies, a person will only be able to request a visit to sick call on specific days. As an example, a prison may make sick call available four days each week—Sunday, Monday, Wednesday, and Thursday, between 6:15 p.m. and 6:45 p.m. In this example, the door for sick call would open at 6:30 in the evening.

A staff member from Health Services would collect prisoner ID cards and issue forms for the men to fill out describing the reason that they're requesting medical attention. People who are not waiting at the door when it is open to receive their forms miss out. By 6:45 a staff member would close the door.

If a person misses sick call, he will need to wait until the next available Sick Call opening. Since prisons typically hold several hundred people, anyone going to sick call should anticipate a long line of others waiting to schedule their own appointments. When a prisoner's name comes up, he will have an opportunity to talk briefly with a staff member to describe the illness. The sick call procedure is simply for screening, not medical treatment.

Except in emergencies, a person may wait between one and three weeks before he is able to meet with a physician. Emergency care is said to be available 24-hours each day. In practice, people in a typical USP, FCI, or prison camp get a different experience.

Tom's Story:

Tom said that he did not have any previous experience with Health Services. While confined in a low-security prison, he said that he began to feel ill on a Monday evening. He had a high fever during the night and felt nauseated when he woke on Tuesday morning.

Tom reported his illness to the officer on duty and requested permission to remain in the unit for rest. The officer didn't authorize Tom to remain in the unit. Instead, the officer quoted policy, mandating him to report to the assigned work detail as scheduled or face disciplinary procedures. In prison, policies frequently trump human interactions.

Tom said he walked the 200 yards that separated his housing unit from his work detail so that he could report on time for duty at 7:30 a.m. He told his supervisor that he felt sick, as if he had the flu, or some type of virus. Tom requested permission to rest in the housing unit. The supervisor told Tom to stay on the job for a few hours to see how he felt. Ninety minutes later, the supervisor allowed Tom to leave.

Since it was a Tuesday, Sick Call wasn't available until the following Wednesday evening. Tom returned to his unit and went to bed. A couple of hours later he had to vomit. After vomiting, Tom went to see the officer in his unit and asked for permission to see a doctor. The officer called Health Services. Rather than agreeing to see Tom, the person at Health Services told the officer to instruct Tom to take some aspirin and report to Sick Call the next Wednesday evening.

Health Services saw only *emergency* cases on days when Sick Call was not available. In prison, staff members define an emergency as being life threatening.

Tom suffered through that day and the next. At 6:10 on Wednesday evening, he walked the 300 yards between his housing unit and the Health Services building. More than 30 people were waiting in line. Since there weren't any seats, he stood waiting for his turn. It was his first visit to Health Services and he didn't know what to expect.

The officer opened the door to collect ID cards and issue forms each person could complete to describe the illness or symptoms. Tom wrote that he been vomiting and feeling weak for two days. When the PA called him, Tom handed his form to the PA.

The PA read Tom's form but didn't ask any questions. He didn't offer advice or prescribe medicine. Instead, the PA gave Tom an appointment to return to Health Services the following Monday morning.

Over the next few days, Tom's illness began to pass. By Monday, the day of his scheduled appointment, Tom felt completely better. He skipped his appointment without seeing anyone from Health Services.

Later that evening, the Lieutenant's office summoned Tom to cite him with a disciplinary infraction. The report accused Tom of being out of bounds because he missed an appointment. When the lieutenant asked Tom why he didn't go to the medical appointment, Tom told him that he felt better and didn't need to see the doctor. When he needed to medical attention, Tom said no one would treat him or give him medicine. The lieutenant told Tom he still had a responsibility to go to the call out.

After his unit team members convicted Tom of the disciplinary infraction, they sanctioned him with the loss of telephone and visiting privileges for 30 days.

Emergency Medical Problems:

Emergency medical problems are different. If there's a sudden and abrupt change in a person's health, staff may send him for emergency care.

Austin's Story:

Austin was 59 when a staff member determined that he needed emergency medical care.

It was winter in the Northeast prison where he was held. After completing his shift working in the kitchen, he walked back to the housing unit. Snow and ice made the ground slippery.

While walking, he slipped and fell down, face first. He broke his nose, two of his teeth, cut his face, and he hurt his legs. Austin needed immediate medical attention. The guard on duty outside the cafeteria saw him fall.

Since Austin fell after regular hospital hours, the guard had to call the hospital for emergency medical attention. Two of Austin's friends picked him up and walked him over to the Health Services Department.

A PA was on duty, but no doctor was available. Austin said the PA provided several Ibuprofen pills and instructed Austin to take the medication. The PA told Austin that the pills would help him with his blood pressure problem. "I don't have a problem with blood pressure," Austin said. "I fell down and hurt my nose, cracked my teeth."

The PA didn't look at Austin's medical file, didn't examine his nose or the pain in his mouth from the broken teeth. The PA sent him back to his housing unit with the Ibuprofen. Austin learned that emergency medical care in prison differed from what he expected.

After the fall, Austin said he never got over the pain. He had to walk with a cane, usually with the assistance of another prisoner. Swelling in his left ankle began soon after his fall, but Austin said Health Services would not treat the problem. They told him that since the ankle swelling wasn't life threatening, Health Services wouldn't treat it.

Patient Requiring Medical Monitoring:

Peter was 66 and he suffered from severe arthritis and diabetes. As a result of his medical condition, Peter said it was hard for him to walk. He'd been incarcerated for a decade, and while at a previous BOP facility, the Health Services Department authorized him to purchase a special pair of boots made for patients who suffered from orthopedic disorders.

Peter paid approximately $350 for his orthopedic boots and he used them for a year. They made walking easier for him. When Peter transferred to a lower-security prison, the Health Services Department at the new prison refused to grant Peter permission to keep his boots. They told him to either donate the boots or send them home.

Despite records showing that he purchased the boots through Health Services at a separate BOP facility, and despite Peter's never having left the BOP's control, staff members said the boots would threaten security of the institution. Instead of the boots, Health Services provided him with orthopedic pads and told him to insert the pads into his prison-issue shoes.

The shoes and pads made walking difficult. Peter said he had to walk with a cane at times, but even that didn't help. His diabetic condition required him to walk several hundred yards each day to the Health Services building for treatment. He also suffered whenever he walked to the cafeteria. Without the orthopedic shoes he needed, Peter said he suffered needlessly. Staff members were indifferent to his pain, he complained.

Peter described a problem he encountered during one of his regular checkups for his arthritic and diabetic condition. About a year ago, when Peter first arrived at his institution, he met with a doctor who completely reviewed Peter's medical file and spoke with him about his illnesses and the treatment Peter had been receiving.

Other than the loss of his orthopedic shoes, Peter said he didn't have any complaints. The doctor prescribed the same medication that Peter had been taking for the past several years. The doctor also prescribed some knee braces to lessen the pain while he walked. Peter saw the same doctor on his next regularly scheduled quarterly visit. The doctor continued the same treatment plan.

At Peter's next quarterly visit, however, a different doctor saw him. The new doctor didn't review Peter's file in front of him and didn't ask about the treatment. Instead, without consultation or explanation, the doctor changed Peter's prescription. He also told Peter that since he'd been using the knee braces for longer than six months, he should turn them in.

Before going to the pharmacy window to pick up his new medication, Peter went to the library to read the *Physician's Desk Reference* (PDR) about the new medicine he was supposed to take. Peter learned that the new medication was for people that suffered from heart problems and hypertension. Peter didn't think he had those symptoms. Peter also learned from his research in the PDR that the new medication might be problematic for those suffering from diabetes.

With this new information, Peter went to the pharmacy window and explained that the doctor must have prescribed the wrong medication because Peter didn't suffer from heart problems.

The pharmacist told Peter he either had to sign up for Sick Call to address those concerns or wait for his next quarterly check-up. The doctor's prescription was final unless another doctor changed it.

Special Surgeries:

Many of the prisoners confined are older and suffer from poor health. Some use Sick Call procedures regularly. They may have to go through emergency care treatment for ongoing illnesses. Some, like Hugh, even proceed through special, major surgeries during their period of incarceration.

Hugh's Story:

Hugh is a 73-year old prisoner who had to go through open-heart surgery. Hugh said he was sick when he came into the system and he believed that he should have been confined in one of the BOP's special facilities for prisoners in need of constant medical attention. Hugh couldn't walk 200 feet without stopping for rest. Since reporting to prison, he's been treated on four separate occasions at outside hospitals for pneumonia.

Tests revealed that Hugh's heart was in bad shape. His left main artery was blocked completely, and the right was 99-percent blocked. As a result of the closed arteries, Hugh's heart didn't receive sufficient blood flow. After tests revealed his condition, guards took him to a community hospital for open-heart surgery. He remained in the hospital for 13 days.

While he was in the hospital, guards shackled both of his ankles to the bed rail. It was particularly painful for Hugh, because the doctors removed veins from Hugh's lower legs in order to replace the blocked arteries. The removal of veins from Hugh's legs left delicate, unhealed wounds. Despite the scars that were developing on Hugh's legs, the cold, steel cuffs were fastened around his ankles every minute of his stay in the hospital. The guards said that policy required the shackles.

The doctors had Hugh breathing through oxygen tanks and argued with the BOP that Hugh needed to remain in the hospital for aftercare and recuperation. It didn't happen. Despite protests, the guards transported Hugh from the hospital back to prison. Hugh spent his first night back in one of the prison's Health Services rooms.

The PA on duty that evening didn't know of Hugh's condition. He refused to provide Hugh with his medication. The officers that transferred Hugh from the hospital back to the prison, apparently, had neglected to provide the changing shift with Hugh's medical paperwork. Hugh tried to explain to the PA that he had just returned from the hospital after having undergone open-heart surgery and that he needed medication because he was in such pain. The PA said he didn't want to hear about it and disconnected the bell that allowed Hugh to call the PA from his room.

The air conditioning in the room blew cold air on Hugh. In response to the cold air, Hugh lifted himself off the bed and went to lie on the floor with his blankets, out of the direction of the cold air that blew on him.

Another officer walked by Hugh's room and saw Hugh lying on the floor. He called a superior to check on him. Hugh explained that he was ill, that the PA was unresponsive to his needs, and that he couldn't return to the bed because it placed his unhealed wounds directly in the path of the cold air. The supervisor located Hugh's medical file, learned of the surgery that he had recently undergone, and made adjustments to Hugh's treatment that evening.

The following day, Hugh returned to his cell in his housing unit. A few hours after Hugh returned to his room, his condition deteriorated. He couldn't control his bowels, became dehydrated, and finally collapsed on the floor.

Hugh's roommate, John, ran to the hospital to notify the staff that Hugh had collapsed and was lying on the floor, unable to move. The PA instructed John to tell Hugh that he should report to Health Services. John stated again that Hugh had collapsed and wasn't able to move by himself. The PA instructed John to bring Hugh over. When John asked for a wheelchair, the PA said Health Services didn't have any wheelchairs. John grabbed a stretcher, located a few other prisoners, and carried Hugh back to Health Services.

A doctor examined Hugh. The doctor determined that Hugh needed to return to the community hospital and summoned an ambulance. Guards chained up Hugh and they drove him back to the hospital. They placed him in the same bed he had been in fewer than 48 hours before. His scarred ankles were again chained to the bed. Hugh remained in the hospital for five more days, during which time the doctors tried to stabilize his condition, feeding him intravenously at first, and then with solid foods.

In general, people going to prison have a better experience if they can toughen up their mindset. They should not have any expectations of a kind, bedside manner or compassion when it comes to health care (or anything else). Instead, they would be wise to expect staff members, in general, to be cynical and to doubt anything a prisoner says.

The Eighth Amendment of the U.S. Constitution requires the government to provide health care services to people in prison. That said, prisoners shouldn't expect to receive the level of care they may be used to receiving outside.

The Health Care department in some prisons will be better than others, depending on resources and the competence of administrators. Some prisons will have different Sick Call procedures than the one described above.

All Health Care departments are challenged to meet the needs of an ever-growing and aging prisoner population. Although the BOP operates seven Federal Medical Centers across the United States, in Butner, NC; Carswell, TX; Devens, MA; Fort Worth, TX; Lexington, KY; Rochester, MN; and Springfield, MO, it struggles to keep up with the medical needs of its swelling and aging population.

The FMCs provide psychiatric treatment and long-term care for the seriously or chronically ill. Apparently, there is not enough space in those facilities to accommodate all the people that need constant medical attention.

Doctors in prison are likely to be overwhelmed by their massive caseloads. As with all staff members, medical doctors in prison "are correctional officers first." Policy will require them to consider security first when treating medical needs.

People in prison would be wise to keep their weight under control, to exercise regularly, and avoid activities that could hurt their medical condition.

Chapter 21

What Should I Know About Food Services and Commissary?

If you heard someone describing their meal in a restaurant as being "about as good as prison food," what would you think?

Keep that thought in mind so we don't have to describe it. Instead, we'll tell you the basics of what to expect.

The good news is that policy requires the Food Services Department to prepare three meals each day for the people in prison. If the prison is operating in accordance with a normal schedule, meaning not on "lock down," at least two of those meals will be hot meals.

In our opinion, food may taste better, with more generous portions, in some prisons than in others. A change in wardens or a change in administrators can change the entire composition of the menu. But overall, as the saying goes, it's all prison food.

The daily food budget per inmate may not be the same in each institution. In penitentiaries, for example, wardens may allocate higher budgets for food. Administrators of those institutions manage a more violent, predatory, and volatile group of men. They may pacify the "institutional mood" by serving more and better food. People inside may receive double cheeseburgers and a mountain of crispy french-fries. They may be able to pass through the food line for second servings. Other prisons do not place as much emphasis on food preparation.

On the low end, administrators may allocate less than $3.00 per day for each inmate, and on the high end, administrators may be able to allocate an average of more than $4.00 per day for each inmate. Rather than budgeting a few dollars for each meal, the per-day budget must cover three meals.

Atmosphere:

More than 8 out of 10 federal prisons serve meals for the general population in a large cafeteria, the *chow hall*. Lines in crowded prisons may take 30 minutes, which limits the amount of time to eat. From the main serving line, men usually continue on to a salad and beverage bar. They sit at two- or four-man tables. In higher security prisons, men segregate themselves in different areas of the chow hall by clique, race, ethnic background, and geographical origins. In low and minimum-security prisons, segregation is less apparent.

Various staff members at the Department Head level or higher are present during each meal in the chow hall. They call it standing *mainline,* meaning staff members are available to respond to inmate questions. A heavy presence of staff keeps a vigilant eye out for "stealing" or moving food from one place to another without authorization. Prisoners should expect staff members to pat search them after any meal. Taking food from the kitchen without authorization can result in a 200-series disciplinary infraction with severe sanctions that include loss of good time and other sanctions.

For people in the SHU, on lockdown, or in prisons without a chow hall, orderlies deliver food at room temperature through slots in the door.

Alan's Story of Mainline:

"I was in the chow hall in Atlanta. The warden stood mainline, and I wanted to talk with him about a problem I was having with the mail. Curly stood ahead of me in the line and I couldn't help hearing what he said to the warden. As always, there were a few other staff members standing around the warden when Curly spoke to him.

Curly says, 'Warden, I got a problem down in the law library. I'm trying to appeal my case and I need a certain citation. The law book with the citation I need has some pages ripped out. I keep telling the librarian, but he never orders the book."

"The warden stood there listening to Curly's complaint. When Curly finished, the warden said to Curly, 'Hold on a minute.' Then he called over a lieutenant. 'Lieutenant' the warden said, 'lock this man up. Send him out to Lompoc, in California.' While the lieutenant was putting hand cuffs on Curly, the warden said, 'Let's hope they have that law book you're looking for out there.'"

After listening to how the warden treated Curly, Alan said he stepped away from the line. Conversations with a warden could bring unanticipated results.

Meal Times:

Staff members operate prisons in accordance with a strict schedule. Every day, the cafeteria opens for meals at the same time—unless there is some type of disturbance.

On weekdays, breakfast usually begins at 6:00 a.m. By 6:30, the loudspeaker will announce "Last Call" over the institutional broadcast system. Prisoners have about ten minutes to make it to the chow hall for their meal after last call.

The lunch meal is usually the most popular meal in the institution. Many people skip the breakfast meal, and some may avoid dinner. The vast majority of people go to the chow hall for lunch.

The chow hall usually starts serving lunch around 11:00 and locks its doors by 1:00. People have the option of going to any of the meals, but more people go to lunch and dinner. As a result of the heavy crowds, prisons release the units in waves. Workers from the UNICOR factory usually eat first. People that work on other details eat next. Finally, those in the housing units are released according to how their unit scored in the weekly sanitation inspection. Staff members rush people through the meals to accommodate the next wave.

After the 4:00 p.m. daily census count, unit officers distribute mail to each prisoner. Once mail has been distributed, the chow hall opens for dinner. It remains open for about one hour.

People in prison get their meals on either plastic trays or plates. They eat with durable plastic knives, spoons, and forks. Sometimes they eat with disposable plastic silverware. The cups are plastic as well. People in prison do not use metal silverware, which could be converted into weapons. Nor do they see much glass or porcelain.

On weekends and holidays, prisons may operate on a different schedule. The chow hall usually opens 30 minutes to an hour later for the breakfast meal, and instead of lunch, the institution serves a brunch meal. Dinner is served at the regular time. On holidays, the meal may be limited to bagged sandwiches and chips.

Food Type:

The Food Service Administrator is responsible for preparing the menu. In our course, we provide sample menus. The sample menu is one part of a five-week cycle. The meals are quite similar during other parts of the cycle, but the days are rotated on which the meals are served. Most institutions allow inmates to choose a soy-meal substitute or cheese if the prisoner does not want to eat meat.

Although food on the mainline may be rationed, larger prisons offer a separate salad bar and "hot bar" from which prisoners are free to eat without limits. Hot bars in some prisons offer beans and rice virtually every day. Salad bars offer combinations of lettuce, spinach, carrots, cucumbers, cabbage, and occasionally other kinds of vegetables. Such options make healthier diets possible.

Gerard's Story:

"I never eat off the mainline. I figure the food served off that line has to be the lowest quality possible for human consumption. Since I'm going to be in prison for over two decades, I'm consciously taking every precaution to preserve my health. I'd hate to get out of here and learn that I have some kind of cancer, influenced by the type of food I've been eating for 20 years. I quit eating all meat and all fried foods. With support from family, I buy cans of tuna and mackerel from the commissary that I bring with me whenever I come to the chow hall. I grab a bowl of rice and beans from the hot bar, and vegetables from the salad bar. Then I mix in my canned fish, and that's my meal.

"Also, since I can't arrange a dental appointment when I want, I don't drink anything but water. No coffee, tea, or sodas. I don't want the stains on my teeth, which I want to keep. A lot of guys in prison lose their teeth, probably because of their diet or hygiene habits. When they open their mouth, you see a black hole, which probably won't help their search for employment when they get out. I'm doing everything I can to minimize the downside of decades in prison."

Preparations:

Staff members direct people that work in the kitchen to bring in the appropriate quantity of food from the warehouse before each meal. Inmates provide all the labor to prepare the meal in accordance with the daily menu—which always is subject to change. Staff oversee rations and discourage people from stealing. They neither cook nor clean. In my book *Lessons from Prison,* I wrote about my experience of having to clean pots and pans for several hours each day when I started serving my term.

While others serve people in the general population from the main serving line, staff members watch every plate closely to ensure that the inmate servers are not providing too much food. In higher-security prisons, less scrutiny is given to the portions. Staff members may have more pressing matters to occupy their time—like avoiding disturbances or mutiny.

Special Meals:

Certain religions require followers to adhere to strict dietary laws. To accommodate these special needs, the BOP makes *common fare* meals available to those who make the choice. Common fare meals, which the BOP purchases from outside vendors, meet kosher and other religious requirements.

Rules prohibit people that choose to eat common fare from eating anything off the mainline or the hot bar. They cannot have a choice from one day to the next. Rather, if they are on the common fare line, they are restricted from the other meal options. Staff will discipline people if they're assigned to common fare but attempt to get food from the serving line. The chaplain signs people up for common fare, but kitchen staff monitor compliance with the program.

Administrators also make provisions for the Muslim inmates that fast between sunup and sundown during the Ramadan season. During Ramadan, Muslim prisoners cannot eat during the regularly served meals. The BOP provides them with meals at times that are in accordance with their religious beliefs. Most institutions also offer one ceremonial meal each year for the various religious groups.

On federal holidays, the BOP traditionally prepares special meals that are far more elaborate than on any other day. People look forward to larger servings selections that aren't available at other times. Christmas and New Year's meals, for example, may include game hens, wild long-grain rice, and layered salads with olives, cheese, and croutons.

On Thanksgiving prisoners can expect turkey, usually in extra-large portions, with stuffing, yams, and cranberry sauce. During the summer holidays, Memorial Day, 4th of July, and Labor Day, administrators may approve "cookouts" with all-you-can-eat barbecue hamburgers and hot dogs. Desserts, also, are much more extensive during the holiday meals.

Commissary:

All prisons operate a commissary. People can purchase food to supplement their diets from the commissary. They can also purchase sneakers, toiletries, and some athletic wear. Our course offers a sample list from a commissary list. The menu of items available vary from one prison to the next.

Besides items on the commissary list, prisoners also may have access to special-purchase orders. Those that participate in arts-and-crafts or hobby-shop programs, for example, will be able to purchase their supplies from outside vendors through the commissary. Some prisons authorize people to purchase special athletic apparel, too.

Each prisoner is given a monthly spending limit in accordance with a national policy, which is adjusted for inflation periodically. Generally, the spending limit does not include items such as stamps, credits for the Inmate Telephone System, or email system.

In theory, a person can make it through prison without any money. But typically, a person needs about $100 a month to get basic toiletries and so forth in prison. On the high end, a person that has access to $600 a month is able to eat and live better in prison. As is the case with anywhere else in America, higher levels of income make life easier.

People cannot shop at will in prison, however. Most institutions assign a specific weekday for each person to shop. Registration numbers will determine the specific day a person can shop.

On his assigned day, the person turns his commissary list in to the commissary officer. A prisoner that works in the commissary gathers items marked on the list. A staff member then charges the inmate's commissary account. Prisoners may replenish their commissary accounts through their prison earnings or from money that others send them from the community.

Those being held in SHU are generally restricted in their access to commissary items.

Besides the commissary, some prisons also make vending machines available. Vending machines may carry sodas, candies, cakes, and food like sandwiches or pizzas that people can heat in unit microwaves. People with financial resources may refrain from eating in the chow hall altogether and gets all of meals from the commissary or the vending machines.

Jake's Story:

"I avoid the chow hall for a reason. It's not that I don't like the food. To be truthful, I never expected much from prison food, so I've never been disappointed. But I've been in a long time.

During the time that I've been in, most of the group problems I've seen began in the chow hall. There are just too many people in one place. Too much tension. Besides that, there is all that searching. I try to avoid the staff as much as possible. If I go to the chow hall, I'm putting myself in their line of sight. There is a good chance an officer will want to search me. Or someone may say something I don't like, putting me in a position of having to respond.

For me, it's easier just to avoid it all. I pay guys who work in the kitchen to bring me vegetables. I mix the vegetables with food I buy from the commissary. Or I buy sandwiches from the vending machine. We all make choices. I choose to avoid the risks that come with the large crowds in the chow hall."

Final Word:

Obviously, food plays a huge role in every person's life. We need food to live, and people in prison rely on administrators to provide it. Food availability varies from one prison to the next. We advise people not to expect much in order to minimize disappointments. Complaining about food is a common pastime in every prison. It unites people in frustration. But it doesn't do much else.

Chapter 22

What Should I Know About the Underground Economy?

Many people go into the prison system with the intention of avoiding all problems and getting out of prison at the soonest possible time.

Every day they have the power to make decisions with regard to how they're going to respond to their environment. They do not have the power to decide how others will respond to the environment. The more they understand about prison, the more they empower themselves to navigate the challenges and complexities successfully.

When judges sentence people to prison, the prisoners become wards of the system. In the BOP, the government assumes control and responsibility for each person's existence. While a person serves time in the BOP, he's deprived of the opportunity to earn a living. The system provides basic needs. Along with a bed, or a mat, the system issues sheets and blankets. People get standard clothing. The men have reasonable access to showers and bathroom facilities. The BOP provides three daily meals. If a person needs medical attention, a process exists for him to follow.

Essentially, the system reduces men in prison to a status equivalent to that of highly dependent child, but without the toys and goodnight kisses.

Adults do not react well to this stripping of independence and responsibility.

Rules do not allow for much in the way of personal possessions. If a person accumulates property—like clothing, nicer sneakers, sunglasses, watches, or radios—that the prison does not issue, staff may confiscate the property as contraband. Staff members may also cite the person with a disciplinary infraction.

Those not mentally prepared for the complexities or prison life may feel their identities being stripped away. Over time, people resent the institution's quest for total control. They do not want to be restricted to wearing only government-issued clothing. They do not want government-issued food. And they do not want to eat only at times dictated by institutional rules.

Rather, like all human beings, people want autonomy over their lives. They want the freedom to make choices. Some people try to bend the system. If they are caught, they should expect punishment that may result in harsher living conditions, or longer stays in prison.

Some people adjust to the rigidity of rules and regulations by creating their own informal bartering system—or underground economy. They create an exchange of goods and services.

This universal aspect of prison life represents one response to the total control that administrators strive to exercise over the lives of the men in confinement.

Through covert exchanges between themselves, people lift some of the monotony that comes with institutional living.

Every day for years at a time, people in prison listen to the same bells that ring at the same time. Rules dictate *where* they are supposed to be, *what* they are supposed to be doing, and *how* they are supposed to be doing it. Regulations dictate what people are supposed to be *wearing* at those times *when* they are supposed to be complying with the machine.

People do not ask *Why* so many rules exist. The monotony machine does not provide answers. A long-term prisoner knows exactly what he will be doing five years in the future because it's the same thing he is doing today. If he has been incarcerated for a while, it may be the same thing he was doing five years ago.

Endless repetition might drive a man to madness if there were no opportunities to bring some variation to his life. Since the prison system does not provide opportunities for much in the way of differentiation, the men create it for themselves through the underground economy. Although a person may choose not to participate in the underground economy, it's wise to understand how it operates.

Cautionary Information:

Every prisoner should realize that the disciplinary code prohibits one inmate from giving anything of value to another inmate. If an individual runs out of stamps, a cellmate is not supposed to lend one; if a new prisoner comes in and does not have a toothbrush, the hard rule is that he must wait until an officer provides it or until he can purchase one from the commissary.

In reality, prison does not work this way. People in prison rely on each other. In doing so, they may violate code 328 of the disciplinary code, which prohibits anyone from:

> "giving money or anything of value to, or accepting money or anything of value from another inmate, or any other person without

staff authorization."

The letter of code 328 indicates that an individual cannot even give a gift to his daughter without staff authorization. People in prison should be aware of the rule.

Administrators want to make it their business to know everything going on in an institution for security reasons. After all, the prison is filled with people convicted of felony crimes.

They recognize that disputes between prisoners can erupt over disagreements. By prohibiting prisoners from exchanging anything of value, administrators limit some opportunities for disagreement. In truth, however, these exchanges between prisoners are as much a part of the life in prison as are the guards themselves. And staff members understand that the underground economy exits.

Currency in the Underground Economy:

Although some people may barter with one another for goods and services of equal value, it's much more common for prisoners to settle their accounts with a currency-like transaction. U.S. currency is considered contraband in prison.

People may use commissary items, such as packs of tuna or candy bars as currency to pay for services. When the value of an exchange exceeds $50, some people settle the debt by having a family member send funds to an address outside of prison. Relatively few people in prison have access to funds outside, however, and they may charge a premium for the service.

A typical federal prison holds about 1,000 men. Administrators require that the people work. We can estimate that, on average, each person in prison earns approximately $30 per month. Some people earn more, many earn less. But on average, it's likely that the system deposits $30,000 into inmate accounts each pay period.

Besides what the prison pays people to work, many people also receive money from home to supplement their income. Family members send money to pay for phone calls, stamps, and commissary items. Although some people do not receive any money from outside sources, others receive more than $1,000 each month to live in prison. On the low side, we think it would be safe to estimate an average of $100 monthly comes into the institution from outside sources for each person in prison.

If those figures are accurate, we could make some assessments. With a typical population of 1,000 men, approximately $130,000 comes through the prisoners' accounts each month. In a larger prison, with more than 4,000 people, more than $500,000 per month passes through inmate accounts. These funds feed and sustain a thriving underground economy.

Indigent Prisoners:

Indigent people in prison play an integral role in the economy. Like everyone else, they have needs that cannot be met through their paltry prison earnings.

BOP policy prohibits some people from earning more than grade four, or approximately $20 per month. Yet the person is required to purchase certain medical items from the commissary if he needs them. If he wants to watch television, he must purchase a portable radio, headphones, and batteries regularly to listen to the sound. Stamps are sold at face value. He may want to purchase toiletries, and even some food from the commissary. If he wants to pay for a phone call, he may need money for that, too. Since prison rules make it difficult for the indigent to survive, many who lack access to outside funds establish themselves in prison *hustles*.

By establishing a hustle, an individual finds a bit of independence from the prison machine. He may perform domestic services like cleaning inmate cells, performing laundry services, or ironing clothes. There is no shortage of opportunities for unskilled individuals to support themselves by providing services for others. Well-heeled prisoners will pay for others to perform services on their behalf.

Most hustlers work so they can earn enough money to ease their own time in confinement. Some, however, are real entrepreneurs and work with hopes of creating a pool of capital that will help them upon their release.

Juan's Story:

Juan is from a poor village in Central Mexico. He was sentenced to a five-year term for his second illegal entry into the United States. He does not speak English and does not have a GED, so his capability for prison earnings is limited. That said, through the services he provides Juan has been able to save an average of more than $400 each month over the past 38 months of his confinement. He has 15 months remaining before his release. If all continues to go well, he expects to have $20,000 in U.S. currency upon his release. With that much capital, Juan says he will be able to set his life up in Mexico far better than he could have had he not come to prison.

Juan begins each morning at dawn. He performs laundry services, three times each week, for two packs of tuna per load. From this service Juan receives between 40 and 50 packs of tuna each week.

Besides the laundry, though, Juan also cleans rooms, for which he charges five packs of tuna per week. Juan earns a total of 30 packs of tuna each week for the six rooms he cleans. During the evenings, Juan irons clothes, for one pack of tuna per item. For ironing services, he earns an additional 30 packs of tuna each week. With all of his domestic services, Juan accumulates approximately 100 packs of tuna each week.

Juan does not eat his tuna, nor does he allow the packs of tuna to sit idly. Rather, he "invests" them. The commissary sells packs of tuna for $1.05 each. But Juan exchange his packs of tuna for $0.85 worth of other commissary items. He accumulates such items as chips, cookies, pastries, and other food products. Juan does not eat these snacks.

Rather, he "runs a store" in the unit. If an individual has a craving for something sweet or runs out of food that he craves, the prisoner can always find what he's looking for from Juan—no matter what time of day or night—as long as the purchaser is willing to return three items for every two items he takes.

Through all of his services, Juan regularly accumulates more than $500 worth of commissary items. He converts that prison currency into cash by selling it for $0.80 on the dollar. In other words, if an individual is willing to send $100 to Juan's mother in Mexico, he will provide that person with $120 worth of commissary. These services keep Juan on track to reach his

$20,000 goal by the time he goes home.

The money will allow him to purchase a dump truck in his hometown. With that truck, Juan expects that he will have the means to build a business through which he can support himself.

With nearly 400 people assigned to each housing unit in this prison, there is no shortage of people who are willing to pay indigent prisoners to make their lives easier. Paying someone through the underground economy is not only about making one's life easier, it's also about avoiding the frustrations and problems that come with prison living.

Although it may be an infraction to give anything of value to another inmate, many people believe that it's wiser to accept this risk and limit one's exposure to frustrations—and more serious disciplinary problems.

For example, there is no shortage of lines in prison. In a large institution, shopping in the commissary requires one to wait around in various lines for at least an hour. There are huge crowds gathered around the commissary. People without resources hang around like leeches, pleading for acquaintances to buy them ice cream or other items.

Shopping in the commissary also puts a person in closer proximity with guards or others that may talk disrespectfully. Those who can afford the fee may avoid commissary frustrations by paying someone else to shop for them. It's not uncommon for family members to send $125 into the account of someone who has no funds. The understanding may be that the recipient of the funds will keep $25 for his own use, and purchase $100 worth of commissary for the person who arranged to have the funds sent.

Corky's Story:

"I haven't shopped in the commissary since my first month in prison. There are too many problems. For one thing, they limit my spending to less than $400 per month. I can't survive on that! The water they sell costs .80 a piece and I go through two of those bottles a day. That's $50 a month right there. I never eat in the chow hall, so it costs me at least $500 for food.

Then there are toiletries and everything else I've got to buy. I also like to keep $100 worth of stamps and packs of tuna around for currency, in case something comes up that I need. I have to pay for someone to cook, to do my laundry, to clean my cell. I even pay a guy to do my job. I'd say it costs me between $800 and $900 each month to live in here, and I'm not carrying anybody.

"It may cost a bit more, but I avoid frustrations that come with all the crowds and the lines. At the commissary, for example, there are so many people hanging around. People I hardly know are hollering out 'buy me this, buy me that.' Some of these guys put a guy in a position where he has to respond. I try to avoid all that.

"Each month, my wife sends a few hundred dollars to a few guys who don't have any money. She has their names and registration numbers. She sends each guy $300. He buys me about $250 worth of goods from the store and he keeps the rest. Hell, they're only earning $20 a month on their jobs, and they don't have anyone outside to help them out. I'm helping them and they're helping me. It works out well for all of us.

"All I'm trying to do is finish up this time and go

home. If I've got to spend a little more to avoid the problems of prison life, so be it. I'm getting a bargain. Every day that I get to avoid the riff-raff of prison is a good day."

Buying Influence:

Administrators like to say that all prisoners are treated equally. Policies require fairness across the board. The reality is that staff members develop better relationships with some prisoners than with others. Through those relationships, individual prisoners in certain positions will build an informal influence, and frequently they will turn that influence into a marketable commodity.

Individuals with influence can be of assistance to others when they are settling into an institution. Some will be helpful in arranging good jobs that meet one's needs, others will assist a prisoner as he struggles to find an agreeable bed assignment. Although there are some prisoners who help as a courtesy, others use their influence as a source of capital. They expect to be compensated whenever they tap into it.

John's Story:

"I was lucky when I came in. I knew Leon from the county jail. By the time I got to prison, Leon had already been settled in for two months. He broke everything down to me on what I could expect as soon as I got out of A&O. I knew that I'd have to get a job, but I didn't know how different the jobs were.

If I were assigned to a job in maintenance, I would have to report for work at 6:30 in the morning, and I'd have to stay there all day. Besides that, I wouldn't be able to use the phone. Leon hooked me up with Trevor, who had the job of head orderly in the unit. There was a long waiting list of guys who wanted to work in the unit. I had my mom send Trevor $50. He arranged for me to move to the top of the list. Instead of being stuck in facilities all day, I just complete what I'm supposed to do, and I'm free to use the rest of my day as I see fit. It works out well for me."

Final Word:

Individual hustles and the underground economy are a part of every prison. We've described some of the ways that prisoners participate in the underground economy to achieve their goals, or to ease some of the pains of confinement.

Besides the services we've described, there are many goods procured through the underground economy. Some contraband exposes people to far more serious disciplinary infractions than what one could receive for giving something of value to another. For example, many prisons have a problem with drugs, with prison-made alcohol, and with theft. People that play a role in such activities may subject themselves to prosecution, which is much more grave than disciplinary action taken by the prison system.

People ought to have a plan while they are serving their sentences. They ought to think of how they can use their time in confinement to grow in some way, on some level. Some may choose to use aspects of the underground economy to achieve their goals. It is an individual choice, as Juan certainly uses it differently from Corky. It is nevertheless important for individuals who are coming to prison to know that the underground economy exists. People should prepare themselves to adjust.

If sending money into the account of another prisoner, be aware of the dangers. Mailroom attendants will vigilantly watch over both the incoming and outgoing mail. It's wise not to discuss transactions over the phone or write about transactions through the mail.

Corky told us of his "technique" for sending money to others. He told the person to write a post card to a friend of Corky's. The friend's address did not appear on Corky's visiting list. When Corky's friend received the letter, he sent $300 and Corky's wife reimbursed the friend later. That way, Corky explained, he didn't send anything to anyone.

Corky didn't realize that although he believed he didn't violate any prison rules because he did not give anything of value to anyone else, if a prison staff member learned of the transaction, Corky could face a disciplinary infraction.

Chapter 23

What's it Like in the Prison Society?

Many movies depict prison life. They help us get a frame of reference about what to expect inside.

In *Con Air,* Nicholas Cage and John Malkovich dramatize a group of super-bad convicts who take over a plane that's transporting them from one prison to another by the U.S. Marshal Service. That type of film may influence perceptions Americans have about prisoners.

The Shawshank Redemption, starring Timothy Robbins and Morgan Freeman, is another popular film depicting prison life. That film hit the big screen in 1994, showing prison life from several decades earlier. Those watching the film will see the underground economy in action. They'll see how relationships develop with different characters.

Tom Hanks has a role in *The Green Mile,* which doesn't show much about prison society, but Tom Hanks gives an excellent performance as a firm-but-fair prison guard, The man playing Percy does an outstanding job at portraying a sadistic guard.

Describing prison in a film is a little like describing anything else in a film. We see parts of the society, but not all of the society. There will always be exceptions in prison, and our team strives to teach others how exceptions can make all the difference.

Different Security Levels:

In truth, films are as accurate about one type of prison as they are inaccurate about another. Most prison films showcase the high-tension life of maximum-security living. Those types of prisons can be volatile, and where there is volatility there is danger. One morning may begin like any other. By nightfall, the prison may be on an indefinite lockdown while guards conduct an investigation on reasons behind bloodshed or an orchestrated disturbance.

With so many people serving multiple decades, life in the penitentiary is subject to *drama,* or major interruptions and disturbances. It's violent. In the past, penitentiaries required prisoners to be 26 or older. Now, however, penitentiaries hold hundreds of offenders who are still in their teens. The long sentences they serve suggest that they're never going to leave. Some people in prison, however, look for other strategies to advance their release dates.

Prig's Story:

"I messed up when I first came in. I started running with a few guys from the neighborhood in the beginning. They introduced me to a guy who used to move a lot of drugs before. He led me to believe that he was still active in the game. Him and me were hanging out and we got to talking. I told him about some connections I had outside, and he agreed to help me out. I figured I'd put two guys together and make a little stash of cash to help me through my bid.

Maybe I could even save something for when I got out. Instead of hooking me up, the guy was working with the feds to bring down his own sentence. He had an agent meet my friends outside. They got busted when they were trying to put a deal together and we all caught new charges. I was only serving five years at first. I finished that term and now I'm starting a brand new 188-month sentence."

Minimum Security Camps:

Camps, on the other hand, do not have the volatility or the violence. Tension is ubiquitous and explosive in a penitentiary setting. In camps, people get along as well as strangers would get along in a large housing development. People are civil and pretty much mind their own business. Few want to be pushed up the ladder of security, so people let a lot of annoyances pass them by in minimum security. In the penitentiary, people are harder, with some people acting as if they're evil incarnate. The majority of men in prison camps are much more contrite, or courteous, in demeanor, just passing the time until they can go home.

With the passage of the First Step Act, we anticipate many more incentives in the federal system. Those incentives will motivate people to work toward earning higher levels of liberty and qualifying for the earliest transition to home confinement.

Bob's Story:

"I was in the camp at Fairton for about nine months. It wasn't nearly as bad as I expected prison to be. The place was clean, the food wasn't bad, and I didn't feel any tension between the guys. If I wanted to avoid someone, I could stay to myself.

"There were fewer than 100 guys serving sentences in the camp and I didn't feel much in the way of harassment from anyone, staff or inmates. With the help of an orderly, I coordinated a job for myself in the library. It was a just a small room with lots of books and I passed my days catching up on reading. I hadn't read at all since I was in college because work kept me too busy. During the time I was at the camp I read about 30 great books and I lost 25 pounds. I'm back down to the same weight I was when I was in school and I feel better than ever. My wife loves the new look. She says the sentence probably gave me an extra ten years to live."

Administrators free up space for new offenders in the penitentiaries by pushing those that qualify for lower security in medium-security prisons. Higher security levels have much higher cost-per-man to operate because of staffing and other measures. As a result of people transferring from penitentiaries to mediums, the atmosphere in medium-security prisons is not much different from that in the penitentiaries.

In mediums, officers regularly find weapons during their shakedowns. Drug and alcohol use is more prevalent. Group disturbances like food strikes, work strikes, and riots are not without precedent. Prisoners in the medium may be serving life sentences and just as serious about their commitment to convict society as their brethren in the penitentiary.

Hector's Story:

"I wasn't feeling the medium-FCI at all. I started my bid behind the gates at USP Pollock. From there I went to the penitentiary at Allenwood. Everything was cool at Allenwood. Then I got a sentence cut and they shipped me over to the medium in McKean, in Pennsylvania. Nothing but a bunch of fake-ass muthafuckas. They say they go hard, but them bitches be tellin' the police everything. The lieutenant came with some of his bullshit at me, and I told him to send me right back to the pen. I wanted serve my time with men, not with a bunch of crybabies."

Low-Security Prisons:

As a rule, low-security prisons now hold men with no more than 20 years remaining to serve. Guys in the low also must have the appropriate security scoring, which generally means they are a less volatile group than those populating the mediums and highs. Administrators try to screen out those in the lows with gang affiliations, or those who have chronic disciplinary problems.

Members of our team have served several years in every type of prison. We've been in penitentiaries and made progress, we've been in mediums and made progress, we've been in lows and made progress, and we've been in camps and made progress. For this reason, we're convinced that people can succeed regardless of where administrators confine them.

Everything depends upon attitude, mindset, and the decisions we make while we serve our time.

In lower-security prisons, a higher percentage of people are closing in on their release dates. With more people preparing for release, there is less volatility, less likelihood for group disturbances. It's easier for a person to avoid trouble with others.

Comparisons:

Prison society differs from society outside. In the broader community, people call the police when they witness a crime. In prison, reporting a rule infraction to staff may expose the person to being abused from others. Each step lower in security brings a person closer to the values that govern society outside of prison.

Higher-security prisons confine people with more time to serve and with more severe histories of violence or disturbance. Even in those environments, if a person chooses a structured schedule and doesn't disrespect others or the tacit rules of prison society (keep your mouth shut and don't interfere with others), a person may avoid altercations.

Prisoners going inside should remember that they're living in a volatile, explosive population that sometimes relieves pressure by acting irrationally. If a person uses critical-thinking skills every day, he becomes better prepared to avoid conflict. People can avoid problems if they choose to avoid problems, but we have to think.

As Stephen Covey wrote in his book The Seven Habits of Highly-Effective People:

» Seek first to understand before seeking to be understood.

By understanding more about how the prison operates, we become more effective at avoiding complications inside.

Census Counts:

Despite vast difference in populations, all prisons have some features in common. For example, all prison hold census counts several times each day.

Although the times for count may be institution-specific, as a general rule, staff require people in the federal system to stand for at least two census counts each day. During most counts, standing isn't necessary.

People should expect to go through several counts each day. One institution, for example, requires staff members to count every person in the institution at midnight, 3:00 a.m., 5:00 a.m., 4:00 p.m., sometime after sundown, and again at 10:00 p.m. Additional counts may take place during heavy fog or emergencies, as defined by the custody staff.

Structure of the Day:

The compound usually opens at 6:00 a.m. Provided there isn't any fog, people are free to leave the housing units and go to the chow hall for breakfast, use the telephones or email, go to the gym or rec yard.

On weekdays, most daytime work details begin at 7:30 in the morning. Prisoners go to their work details or various callout appointments. Those who miss the work call or callout may receive an incident report for being out of bounds.

At 8:00 a.m., the shift changes for many staff members. Officers walk through the housing units to ensure that the orderlies are performing their work, that beds are made, and that no one who is supposed to be working is loitering around the unit.

Camps have "open movement," meaning people may walk around freely. In secure institutions, some form of *controlled movement* exists.

With controlled movement, people need to wait for a specific time, or get a pass, to move from one area of the compound to another. It's like a pass that children in primary school use when they want to leave the classroom to go to the library or bathroom. Ordinarily, officers begin issuing passes after their 8:00 a.m. rounds in the housing units.

In medium and high-security prisons, the controlled movement procedures are substantially more rigid. Passes only authorize a person to move from one specific place to another.

For example, a pass may allow a person to move from the housing unit to the library. The window of time to get from one area to the other may be ten minutes, and they may only be authorized to make the move on the hour or on the half-hour.

Most institutions have a "yard recall" at various times each day. During yard recall, all people return to their assigned areas.

At 11:00 a.m., different segments of the prison will be released to the chow hall for the noon meal. People assigned to work details eat first, and they usually have a 30- to 45-minute window before they report back to work details. Detail supervisors will take a roll call at both 7:30 and after the men return from lunch. Spontaneous roll calls also take place throughout the day. Some staff make a real effort to catch prisoners out of bounds. They take disciplinary action against those who not in their assigned area.

By 1:00 p.m. most chow halls close. As long as the men are not working, they may use the library facility, the recreation facility, or walk around the recreation yard. In institutions with open movement, prisoners may walk around freely at any time except count times and when the facility is locked down.

Around 3:30 in the afternoon, most institutions have a recall, requiring people to return to assigned quarters or work details. There will be a staff shift change and a count. When the count clears, officers distribute mail in the housing units. After mail call, the units will be released for the evening meal.

After the evening meal, most people in the prison have a modicum of free time, depending upon security level. After 8:00 pm, prisons tend to shut down, requiring the people to stay in the housing unit. They may watch television and use the telephone or email system.

Basically, people in prison schedule their lives around times that the institution sets for them.

Inmate-Staff Relations:

As we've written earlier, the BOP has a motto: all staff members are correctional officers first, and they should treat inmates in a firm but fair manner. The vast majority of staff members follow this edict. Generally, they do not form close bonds with people in prison. In higher-security prisons, there may be minimal interactions between staff and people serving time. As men move lower in security, tensions between the two groups lessen.

People in low security, for the most part, recognize the vast majority of staff members as people who are just doing their jobs. For their part, most staff are indifferent to the people in prison. This is not to say they are lax in their duties. Many are eager to write disciplinary infractions for the most trivial of rule violations. On the other hand, if a person is respectful of authority, uses good critical-thinking skills, and doesn't bring problems, he is likely to serve his sentence without too much interference.

Staff members are responsible for maintaining order in the institution. They regularly search people and spaces. They may speak pejoratively to a prisoner, too. A person has to let those remarks slide off. They are a part of prison life, just as living with loud and disrespectful people is part of prison life. If a person can keep cool in the face of adversity, the chances are good of making progress and preparing for a successful return to society.

Gangs:

Staff in higher-security prisons sometimes have problems with prison gangs. These are prisoners who come together as groups formed along racial, ethnic, or geographical lines. They are like pseudo families, with leaders and "soldiers" that come together, usually in solidarity in an effort to control some of the illicit activities inside the institution.

These include drug rackets, gambling, loan sharking, extortion, prostitution, debt-collections, and hits. Some gangs are predatory in nature, and present problems because they have members throughout the prison system. If a person has problems with one gang member, he may have problems with all the members of the individual's gang. In this way, violence between gang members easily spills over into the general population.

Gangs are a fact of life in high-security prisons. A 1994 study by the American Correctional Association estimated that there were more than 46,000 gang members in the federal system and in the prisons of at least

35 states. To put this number in perspective, consider that there were fewer than 150,000 people in federal prison at the time.

Administrators consider gangs an extreme menace to prison management. Those that affiliate in any way with gangs may expect harsher treatment from the system. If a person has aspirations of moving to lower-security level institutions, or taking advantage of the First Step Act, he ought to avoid even the appearance of gang association. Low-security prisons have much lower problems with gangs, and in camp, gangs are nonexistent.

Those sent to higher-security institutions will want to avoid attracting attention. If they have access to outside funds, they should not flaunt it. Penitentiaries are full of predators who keep an eye out for everything. They watch to see who is receiving mail, and who is regularly shopping in the commissary. One can avoid attention by accepting a regular job, choosing one's associates carefully, and staying away from the three cardinal sins of prison:

- No gambling,
- No drugs, and
- No homosexual activity.

Most important, prisoners should mind their own business. Always.

To avoid problems, people should realize that everyone is separated from loved ones. For that reason, there's a 24-hour tension. Some people don't respond well to courtesy, or to seeing others visibly at ease. To the extent possible, try to live as a stoic. In higher security, try not to express too much emotion, and be unmoved by either joy or grief. Don't allow noise, violence, or the behavior of others to disrupt inner peace.

Understand all the complications that can follow an inappropriate response to a problem. Remember that dynamite comes in small packages.

In other words, don't get involved in every annoyance, because the consequences may result in harsher conditions or a longer time in prison.

Cliques:

Frequently people stick together in small cliques of anywhere from three to five members. They may have similar interests, enjoy eating together, exercising together, and just passing time in each other's company.

Within a group of 1,000 men, people are bound to find others with whom they're compatible. These relationships can be healthy, providing a sense of friendship in an atmosphere where it's easy to feel alienated from the broader community.

Groups:

Some people pass time by participating in groups that are active in one of the many programs inside. Religious groups, for example, bring the men together on a daily basis for prayer or worshipping services.

It is not uncommon to see these men embrace one another whenever they meet, or shake hands each time they come together.

Prisoners tend to form a camaraderie with others who come from similar social backgrounds, educational backgrounds, or geographic locations. No man has to serve his time alone, although a small percentage of people limit themselves to interacting with only a handful of others.

Final Word:

The security level of the institution will be the most significant factor in shaping the particular prison society.

Higher-security institutions will be more volatile than lower-security institutions, and camps will basically be absent of both volatility and violence. We anticipate the First Step Act will also influence more people to avoid problems, as they will want to qualify for maximum incentives and Earned Time credits.

There's a myth among people outside that homosexual rape is a common occurrence in prison. It happens far less frequently than rumor has it. As with all cases of violence, it's more prevalent in higher security institutions. Even there, prison rape occurs relatively rarely during a given year. It happens, just not as frequently as rumor suggests.

In the federal system, staff members keep a vigilant eye on the population. Not only are staff members present throughout the institution, but numerous video cameras are placed in plain view in all housing units and around the prison compound.

Chapter 24

How do I
Stay Connected with Society?

In earlier lessons, we described a criminologist's theory about adjustments in prison. He theorized that adjustment patterns in prison follow a U-shaped graph.

People hold close ties to society when they are coming into the metaphorical "U." As they approach the center of their sentence, perspectives shift. Their values and behaviors tend to blend with those of the prison society. Then, as the individual moves closer to the end of his sentence, he begins ascending the right vertical side of the "U." Perspectives shift again. He leaves the culture and values of the prison society behind and identifies with the value patterns of the community he will return to after release.

I felt that pattern, even though I served an 18-month term for securities fraud. Surrendering to prison, leaving behind my family, my dog, my friends and career really hurt. As I moved into the midway point of the term, I adjusted well. I was exercising, writing, preparing for the career I wanted to build. Then, I started to inch closer to my release date, I started to feel that anxiety again, eagerly awaiting my liberty.

Prison changes the way people think. People who never experienced confinement make the mistake of identifying a prisoner's disciplinary record as an indication of his preparation for living in society. Staff members may say that a person who received a single disciplinary infraction—no matter how trivial—obviously has not learned right from wrong. After a person lives inside for a while, he recognizes that blemished disciplinary records are often symptomatic of the prison system's poor design.

People outside of prison may not think of paying someone to "steal" food from the kitchen. Inside, life is different. For some, buying vegetables and fruit from kitchen hustlers becomes as common as brushing one's teeth.

As a person passes time inside, it's easier to be more temperate in our judgment of others going through the prison experience. After a few years inside, a person that once led a professional career may talk about a 12-month sentence as being insignificant. Before going to prison, people may think a year in prison would be life altering. As time passes, the prison term feels less unsettling, possibly because everyone in the community serves time.

The longer a person serves, the more susceptible he becomes to being conditioned by the system. A man who enjoyed a rich social life outside, filled with family, friends, and business acquaintances, may go through a meltdown period. As holidays pass, a person may sense the loss more acutely. Out of site out of mind. Mail comes less frequently.

For many, money to buy commissary becomes a problem. Outside resources get depleted. These factors of prison life tend to push people deeper into the abnormal society that exists behind prison fences. Unless people make conscious efforts not to do so, they begin to pick up the prison vernacular. They embellish sentences liberally with vulgar and profane language. Some become skillful at understanding the rules—not so they can abide by them, but so they can navigate their way through them without being caught.

Prisons can make a person feel as if he's lost hope and control over his own destiny. As people move deeper into their sentences, they may feel more separated from society. After a few years pass, they might only be able to communicate with other people in prison. People in prison can lose touch with the society outside of prison fences if they don't take action.

Unfortunately, a common myth in many prisons is that the easiest way to serve time is to leave outside society behind as they enter the prison. The problem with that theory is that the more a person conditions himself to live in prison, the more he simultaneously conditions himself to fail in society.

My partner, Michael Santos served 26 years in prison. Rather than separating himself from society, he made conscious, deliberate efforts to grow stronger in every way. As a result of his daily efforts to connect with others, he succeeded in opening relationships. Those relationships led:

» To bringing mentors into his life,

» To earning a bachelor's and a master's degree

» To publishing several books,

» To his coordinating friendships with numerous business leaders,

» To his building multiple income streams, and

» To his getting married during his 16th year of imprisonment.

Instead of struggling upon release, Michael launched a lucrative career. In *Earning Freedom: Con-*

quering a 45-Year Prison Term, Michael attributed his success to rejecting that myth that adjusting in prison requires a person to forget about the outside world. Efforts he made to connect with law-abiding citizens opened numerous opportunities for him, and he urged others to do the same.

In our opinion, people ought to work toward maintaining close ties with society. That strategy worked well for our partner Shon and it worked well for me. Shon developed mentor relationships that had a huge influence on his ability to launch his career upon release.

Instead of lamenting over lost relationships, make efforts to forge new ones. Create a strong support network. Strong relationships help people overcome challenges and obstacles upon release.

The BOP publishes policies indicating that it encourages people to maintain close ties with the community. Those statements tend to belie policies by which people have to live in prison. For example, as a general rule, prisoners are not allowed to visit with people they did not know prior to incarceration. Another rule limits people from the amount of time they can spend on the telephone. Further, disciplinary sanctions frequently include taking telephone and visiting privileges away.

> *As a disclaimer: We're writing this book prior to full implementation of the First Step Act, which may open opportunities for people in prison to build mentor relationships.*

People should expect obstacles as they try to connect with society. It makes sense to invest time and energy to grow in spite of such barriers.

Many people get depressed during confinement. They lose focus, or have a hard time completing activities that they used to accomplish routinely—like reading a book, studying, exercising, or sleeping. They just get sad and vegetate. They have built an idea of their worth as a human being according to the success, accomplishments, or life they lived prior to prison.

For those that fail to take action, prison distorts a self-image. Confidence can slip away, resulting in a debilitating depression.

Our team argues that leading a values-based, goal-oriented adjustment can make all the difference. It can empower people. Prison provides an excellent opportunity to sublimate energy and develop new skills. Pursuing meaningful goals in the midst of struggle can boost self-esteem. Consider:

- Working to build or develop a stronger vocabulary,
- Learning a foreign language,
- Writing a book,
- Losing weight,
- Earning credentials, or
- Developing new skills.

To succeed in prison, as anywhere else, master the environment. If a person lets the environment master him, depression can set in.

Visiting Policies:

In order to receive visits in federal prison, each person must mail a form to his prospective visitor. The prisoner's counselor provides the visiting form. Once received, the prospective visitor fills out every blank, then returns the form directly to the counselor.

The counselor will search a federal database to check on whether the proposed visitor has been truthful about reporting a prior criminal record. A prior criminal record will not necessarily preclude a person from being added to a visiting list. But if a prospective visitor lies on a visiting form, and the counselor notices, the lie may end consideration for the visit.

If the counselor approves the application, he will update the visiting list. Prospective visitors should send visiting forms through certified mail; it's not uncommon for counselors to say that they did not receive a visiting form. With a return receipt, a person can show the counselor who signed for the form and it may be tracked down.

Two weeks may pass or longer may pass before a counselor updates a visiting list with new visitor. A person in prison should get confirmation that the counselor has approved a visitor prior to requesting the visit. Family members may be added more quickly than two weeks if they're listed on the pre-sentence investigation report.

People new to the system should provide visitors with accurate information on:

» Route to the prison, which they can get from prisoners,

» Days and times of the week that visiting is authorized,

» Advise visitors to bring rolls of quarters for use in vending machines—a good rule is about $10.00 per person,

» Remind visitors to bring picture identification, along with the prisoner's name, housing unit, and registration number,

» Advise visitors on dress code: no colors that match prison uniforms (khaki, green, or orange), no colors that match staff colors (gray), no sleeveless shirts, no sweat pants, no open-toed shoes for women, nothing too provocative or revealing,

» Women may bring a clear plastic bag or baggie to hold change, but purses, handbags and diaper bags are generally not allowed into the visiting room.

By providing prospective visitors with as much information as possible, prisoners lessen some of the hassle associated with prison visiting.

In most institutions, prisoners are limited to 10 non-family visitors and 10 family visitors on their approved list. But they may remove and add visitors by submitting new lists to their counselor. Making frequent changes to visiting lists causes more work for counselors, and they're not always appreciative.

In county jails, visits may take place through a window with a telephone device. Most federal prisons, on the other hand, offer contact visits. It's like visiting someone at a bus station, or an airport. Seats are assigned.

Visiting rooms in camps are easier, allowing people to sit in movable chairs around tables, or even on outside grounds. Most prisons with security ratings higher than camps have theater-style seating in the visiting rooms, and no tables. That means prisoners sit in parallel lines, side-by-side, and shoulder-to-shoulder with their visitors.

After a while, it's not uncommon for the seating arrangement to cause neck aches, as the people have to look to their sides in order to talk.

Rules allow people to embrace and kiss their visitors at the beginning and at the end of the visit. During the visit, prisoners may be allowed to hold hands. They are not allowed to kiss during the visit.

Cameras are placed at strategic locations throughout the visiting room and guards constantly roam around the room keeping a vigilant eye for behavior they consider inappropriate.

Many will not hesitate to terminate visits for the slightest violation of visiting-room rules. If children run around the room without adult supervision, the guards may issue a warning, or they may terminate the visit.

Prisoners should instruct their visitors not to bring anything when they come except a picture ID and change to sodas, chips, cakes, and sandwiches from a bank of vending machines.

Visitors should not dress too provocatively. If staff members think a woman is dressed inappropriately, they may deny entry into the room. Skirts must not be too short, and clothing should not be too tight. It's a good idea to dress as if going to church, or on a job interview.

In secure prisons, officers will strip searched people in prison before and after the visit. Prisoners in camps might not be searched at all. Except in rare instances, staff members will not search a person coming to visit a prisoner. The exceptions are when they suspect the visitor may be trying to smuggle contraband.

Prisons in busy, metropolitan areas generally limit the quantity of hours a person may spend in the visiting room during a given month. Many systems rely upon "visiting points" to control the amount of time a person can spend in the visiting room.

On weekdays, each hour the prisoner spends in the visiting room may count as one point; on weekends and holidays, every hour may count as two points. Administrators may further limit weekend visits by only allowing people to spend alternating weekend days in the visiting room. Every prison has its own visiting rules. People learn institutional rules and visiting times on their first day inside.

Inmate Telephone System:

The Inmate Telephone System (ITS) strictly controls telephone access. Staff members monitor all calls. Sanctions for violating rules may be severe. As always, it's best to know the rules and follow them assiduously. Staff members are quick to impose sanctions when it comes to telephone use, or anything that connects people to society.

Whenever a person makes a call, an automated recording interrupts a few times to announce that the call is from a person in prison. As with visiting lists, counselors will authorize access to the telephone. People may pay for calls by purchasing credits from the commissary. Every person in prison will have his own Personal Identification Number (PIN). In order to place a call, the person uses the PIN, which creates a call record that staff monitor. Staff members monitor all calls on the ITS system with surveillance equipment.

Again, penalties for violating any rules of the ITS system are *extremely* severe. The telephone represents a primary link between many people in prison and their families. Yet for any type of disciplinary infraction that involves a prison telephone, the prisoner should expect to lose his telephone privileges (and perhaps his visiting and commissary privileges, too) for extended lengths of time.

One of the common offenses is the three-way call. That may be a regular feature outside of prison. The BOP's perception of a three-way call is that it's equivalent to a capital offense. Another is using the phone to violate any of the prison's rules. For example, using the phone to instruct someone outside to send money to another prisoner's account. Or using the phone to conduct a business. Prisoners should not discount the seriousness of telephone violations, because penalties are severe.

Like anywhere else, it's best to anticipate problems *before* they surface. If a person has financial interests outside, it's best for the person to create a well-informed strategy long before surrendering to prison.

We recommend that people learn rules and learn what has worked for others, then coordinate a plan of action with people they trust.

If a person needs to have "business conversations," it's best to talk with an attorney first. Then have the attorney contact the BOP for a written opinion on whether certain discussions are authorized over the phone.

Do not engage in business discussions (including stock sales or even the transfer of money from one account to the other) without having a clear, and preferably written understanding of what staff members will permit. People in prison should expect staff members to monitor all telephone conversations.

Melvin's Story:

Melvin waited in the county jail to be sentenced. The county jail did not have a restriction on three-way phone calls. He made them regularly to communicate with his family. After he received a 20-year sentence, the county jail placed him in segregation while Melvin waited for transfer to a BOP facility.

He waited in SHU for five weeks, without access to the telephone. Then the U.S. Marshals picked him up and transferred Melvin to prison. When he arrived, however, administrators learned that they did not have his PSR. As a result, instead of placing him in the A&O Unit, then sent Melvin to SHU. He waited in SHU for a week before his counselor told Melvin that his PSR had arrived and he would transfer to the general compound.

"I haven't spoken with my family for almost two months. Can I make a phone call?" Melvin asked his counselor.

"Sure. I'll issue you a PIN number, but you'll have to submit a phone list. Give me a list of numbers and I'll make sure your phone account is activated by tomorrow."

"But I don't have my property with me and won't know all the phone numbers I want to add to my list until I receive my phone book."

"That's no problem," the Counselor answered.

"Just give me the numbers you remember. When you receive your property, give me a new list to add to it. You're allowed a total of 30 phone numbers on your list."

Melvin transferred to the A&O unit the following day. He called his mom. While talking with her, he asked her to connect him to his sister. His mother made the connection.

Later that evening, a lieutenant paged Melvin. The lieutenant read Melvin his Miranda rights, then told him that he was being charged with making a three-way phone call. Melvin said that it was his first day on the compound. No one told him he couldn't make three-way calls. The lieutenant said the matter would have to be referred to the Unit Team, and then the disciplinary hearing officer.

The following day, Melvin went to the Counselor who had activated his telephone account. He explained that no one had warned him about not making three-way calls, and the Counselor realized that because Melvin was in the SHU, he had missed the A&O presentation which detailed the rules of the ITS.

"Don't worry about it," the Counselor said. "I'll leave a note with the DHO stating that you had not yet gone through A&O when you made the call."

Melvin then went before the Disciplinary Hearing Officer. When he did, the DHO asked Melvin one question—whether he made the three-way call. Melvin admitted that he did. When he tried to explain, the DHO cut him off, saying he didn't want to listen. The DHO found Melvin guilty of the violation. He sanctioned him to loss of telephone privileges for one year, loss of visiting privileges for six months, and loss of commissary privileges for 90 days.

Melvin was beginning a 20-year sentence. He had a seven-year old daughter who didn't understand why her father quit calling, and why she couldn't visit him any longer. When Melvin tried to explain that to the DHO, the DHO told him that he should have thought about his daughter before he was convicted.

Melvin's sanction is not uncommon or particularly harsh when it comes to violations of the ITS. If Melvin were to receive a second violation for a telephone infraction, he would receive the same sanctions, in much longer increments.

Many people in prison have lost telephone privileges for five years. Since telephones and visiting are considered a privilege, and not a right, people should make every effort to understand every rule concerning the ITS completely before they find themselves ensnared in a problem as Melvin did.

If a person is caught using a cell phone, they likely will transfer to a higher-security prison, and they may be charged with new criminal conduct. They will likely be denied access to telephone and visits for several years.

Correspondence Policies:

In most cases, people in prison have a Constitutional right to mail. It is only in the rarest of instances when BOP officials or the courts deny a person access to mail. For many, mail is their primary means of communicating.

They may use the U.S. Postal Service, or they may use the Corrlinks email system.

The Corrlinks, or Trulincs system, is a quasi-email system that is available to people in federal prison. We call it a "quasi" because Corrlinks differs from email people have become accustomed to in the broader society.

As with telephone systems, people must submit names and contact information for people with whom they want to communicate through Corrlinks. Staff members will authorize the communications. Once approved, people in prison can send digital messages through the system. Staff members or an automated system will scan the message. After a couple of hours, the message gets sent to a Corrlinks server. Intended recipients can check the server. They access the message through Corrlinks.

Corrlinks does not have the same instantaneous speed as email, but it's a much more efficient way to stay connected than the U.S. Postal service.

In order to receive regular mail, prisoners must sign a form indicating that they authorize staff members to open and inspect all incoming mail before it is delivered to the inmate. The only mail that may be delivered to the inmate without having been previously opened must be properly marked on the outside of the envelope as legal mail.

Once an individual arrives at his particular institution, he should check with his Unit Team or the mailroom to find the exact rule on what that institution considers "appropriately marked" legal mail; policies vary from one institution to another.

Generally, staff members will not open mail if it adheres to the following guidelines:

» Law firm name on return envelope

» Personal lawyer's name written above law firm name (may be hand written), identifying him as a lawyer,

» Clearly marked "Legal Mail: Open only in the presence of [inmate name and number].

Prisoners may not send or receive packages without written authorization from the Unit Team. If an envelope weighs more than one pound, mail room staff will consider the envelope a package. They may reject the package if it does not include a prior authorization. For that reason, when ordering books, it's best not to order more than two at a time. Further, regarding books and magazines, they should come from a bookstore or publisher.

In high, medium, and administrative-security facilities, prisoners must send outgoing mail in unsealed envelopes. They should expect staff members to read through the mail before they seal and send the mail. In low and minimum-security institutions, people may seal their outgoing mail. But all mail may be inspected and read prior to leaving the institution.

Regardless of a prison's security-level, if a person is not under some type of exceptional mail limitation, he will be able to send mail to his attorney, the court, media representatives, or government officials in a sealed envelope. This type of mail is sent through a *special mail* outgoing mailbox. Staff members will not inspect mail sent from that box unless they have reason to suspect wrongdoing.

Although people in prison may send and receive mail to people in the community, rules prohibit them from writing to people in other prisons unless they have prior authorization. In order to correspond with people in other prisons, both prisoners must receive approval from the wardens of their respective institution. It is not uncommon for wardens to grant permission for family members to correspond, but both people in prison need approval before corresponding.

Final Word:

Staying connected with society is of vital importance. People should create opportunities to build new relationships with law-abiding people during their confinement. For many, the alternative is bad. They may live in prison for years. When they return to society, they may be completely out of step with the world. There is a scene in *The Shawshank Redemption* about one character who finally makes it out of prison after having served a lengthy term. Finding himself unable to cope, he hangs himself.

With 2 million people serving time in American prisons, confinement does not present quite the same stigma in many social circles that it has in decades past. Prisoners should reach outside the fences at every opportunity that comes. In fact, they should do more. In order to prepare themselves, they ought to make conscious efforts to invite new people into their lives. Communicating with law-abiding citizens represents one of the best methods for people to grow, even while growing through struggle.

Chapter 25

How do I Avoid Problems and Make Progress?

Our team strongly recommends people begin preparing for success at the earliest possible time. It's never too early, and it's never too late to sow seeds for a better outcome. And there are always steps a person can take.

Shon may not have known that he was going to become a lawyer when his judge sentenced him to more than a decade in prison. Michael did not know he would begin building a real estate portfolio worth millions of dollars within months of concluding his prison term. And when my judge sentenced me for securities fraud, I certainly did not know that I would be building a consulting practice, nonprofit, and a digital marketing firm right after my release.

The preparations we make early put us on a pathway for success after struggle.

What does it mean to succeed upon release? To some it means becoming a viable, contributing member of law-abiding society. That appears to be a high hurdle for many people who leave prison. When we define recidivists as those individuals who were arrested again within five years after their release from serving a prison sentence, recidivism rates in this country exceed 50 percent. That means more than one out of every two people in prison can expect to have problems with the law again after their release from confinement.

People coming into the system ought to be cognizant of those high rates of failure. They should prepare to ensure that they are a part of the minority of men who are not *prisonized*— conditioned by the system to fail.

Sociologists use the term prisonization to define trying to blend in with the prison society. They adopt the norms and values of the men around them. Many of those norms and values are completely at odds with the values that exist in society.

In maximum-security prisons, for example, people earn respect by developing fierce reputations. Many project images as having zero tolerance for any type of abuse, and they're willing to take any problem to the wall. As some say, it's easy to get respect in prison, as long as the person is willing to pay the price. That price, of course, may result in life in prison. Such attitudes are not restricted to maximum-security.

Blake and Fly's Story:

Blake had only been in prison for a few months when he was confronted with a problem. At the time, he had a few years remaining to serve. He had been assigned to the top bunk in a 12-man room. Fly slept beneath him. One morning, around 6:00 a.m., Blake was climbing onto his top bunk. He farted. Fly was offended at Blake's rudeness and the two men fought.

Fly was getting the better of Blake. Sensing that Fly was taking his manhood, Blake pulled out a weapon he manufactured previously. With a razor, he started slicing Fly's face as if he were dicing a tomato. Had Blake found an artery, he certainly would have killed Fly. Instead, Blake's slices just made crisscrosses across

Fly's face, from forehead to chin, ear to ear, and across his eyes.

Staff members called an ambulance for Fly to go a local hospital. Staff sent Blake to the SHU and he faced criminal charges that will add significantly to his sentence. Some may think this started because one man farted while climbing into bed at 6:00 in the morning. In reality, both men chose how to respond. Their response resulted in a sad ending for both men.

Prison is an unnatural world that can strip away life as a person knows it. The less prisoners expect while living in confinement, the easier it is to move through the term. When people make the mistake of associating their manhood, their honor, their dignity, with how others perceive them in prison, they move closer to prisonization. The more they move into that trap, the more vulnerable they make themselves to enhancing their problems and prolonging their stay in confinement.

To avoid problems in prison, work toward maintaining and building close contacts with society, keep a stable personality, refuse to become a part of a group, and focus on goals. Those who want more out of life than a prison reputation ought to exercise personal discipline and avoid confrontations.

Rudy's Story:

Rudy came to prison with a 13-month sentence. He was well spoken. At first glance, no one would think of him as a person with criminal values. During his first week in prison, Rudy walked into one of the vacant television rooms. It was 6:00 in the morning and he wanted to pass an easy 20 minutes watching the early morning news until it was time for him to report to work. The sign on the door of the TV room said "General TV Viewing." Rudy didn't perceive any problem with what he was doing.

Ironhead walked into the room at 6:10. Disregarding Rudy, Ironhead changed the channel. He watched rap videos, he said, every morning in that room. "Well, you're not going to watch rap videos in here today," Rudy told him. "I'm watching the news." Rudy changed the channel back to the news.

Rudy said that he wouldn't have come off so assertively, but Rudy sensed that he couldn't allow Ironhead to bully him.

"Man fuck all that," Ironhead got in Rudy's face. "This is the video room and I'm a watch videos."

"The sign on the door doesn't say 'Video Room,' Rudy objected. "The sign on the door says 'General Viewing.' I'm watching the news."

Apparently, Ironhead didn't know how to respond to this frail white guy standing up to him. He didn't change the channel. Instead, Ironhead started playing his radio so loud that the thump, thump, thump was blasting through the headphones so that Rudy couldn't watch television.

"Would you turn that down," Rudy said. "I'm trying to watch the news."

"Tough shit white boy," Ironhead said. "You're in jail. Get used to it."

At 6:20, Rudy had to leave the room to report to his job assignment in the kitchen.

Rudy put himself into a volatile situation, one that

easily could have been avoided. Although some would have admired his brass-balls response to Ironhead. They didn't appreciate the risk to which Rudy exposed himself. Rudy responded in the way he did because, as he said "I didn't want to leave Ironhead with the impression that I could be bullied." As a newcomer to the prison, Rudy didn't anticipate where his actions could have led him.

People coming to prison ought to realize that other prisoners develop a sense of entitlement, or ownership, to the most trivial matters. Hardened people in prison may consider a particular metal folding chair, control of a television room, an individual job to be worth fighting to protect, with weapons if need be. Having lost everything of any value in their lives, many people in prison tend to form a link with the inanimate object.

When another person encroaches on property or a situation that a *prisonized* prisoner believes is his own, the altercation can escalate into a battle that should be "taken to the wall." If someone else had been in the room when Rudy stood his ground with Ironhead, Ironhead may have felt that Rudy had challenged his manhood. It could have provoked a violent response from Ironhead.

Fortunately for Rudy, nothing happened. But Rudy could have avoided the situation altogether without sacrificing any of his own self-esteem. At the same time, he could have given Ironhead the "respect" that he craved. When Ironhead said that he used the TV room every day to watch rap video, Rudy could have said, "I'm on my way to work anyway. The room is yours." After all, Rudy wasn't really so determined to watch the news. He just didn't want to be bullied by Ironhead.

People in prison need to develop and use strong critical-thinking skills, considering strengths and weaknesses, opportunities and threats—the well-known SWOT analysis before each decision.

Regardless of how things went down with Ironhead, nothing short of violence would change the way others in prison perceived him. Rudy was white, polite, and courteous. He had no tattoos and all of his teeth. To most hard-core prisoners, Rudy represented the establishment that they feel oppressed them for their entire lives.

In the real world, Rudy runs his own company and he plays an integral role in eight-figure deals. When people like Rudy come to prison, they may want to keep the lives they lead outside in perspective. That's where they expect to return. Most of the people in prison, on the other hand, come from disadvantaged backgrounds. They are more accustomed to prison life, or the culture of confinement.

Just as Rudy could never become accepted in prison society unless he denigrated himself to talking in their vernacular and behaving in ways that prisoners "respect," neither could many of the prisoners ever lift themselves up to the world in which Rudy moves outside. Rudy is best to leave the prisons to the Ironheads, and keep his eyes firmly focused on his 13-month release date.

Coping with Prison Frustrations:

It is inevitable that people experience frustrations while serving time. They may encounter staff members on power trips. They will share bathroom facilities with prisoners who have the sanitary habits of a rodent. They will miss career opportunities because of prison rules. And they may receive bad news from home.

All of these factors are inevitable.

When coming into the system, people need to exercise discipline. They should prepare mentally for what is to come and to keep in mind the words of Fleetwood Mac:

"Don't stop thinking about tomorrow."

Larry's Story:

Larry received an eight-year sentence for money-laundering charges. After sentencing, he surrendered to serve his time at the federal prison camp in Pensacola, Florida. When he arrived, he received a great job on a military golf course. Then Larry received news that his mother died.

When the BOP thwarted his plans to attend the funeral, Larry flipped out. A few days later, he walked away from the camp, trying to begin his life as a fugitive. Several weeks later he was picked up again. As a consequence, authorities charged him with a new crime for escape. Further, his actions implicated his wife and she also received a fresh prison term. Now, because he adjusted poorly to a situation over which he had no control, Larry not only extended his own stay in prison, but he served it in a more restrictive institution. Further, he now lives with the guilt of having caused his wife to serve time, too.

People should accept that factors will present themselves during a term that are beyond a person's sphere of control. When they accept this reality, they feel free to walk away from potential conflicts that can exacerbate problems.

One strategy our team members used to minimize prison stress was pursuing goals. When we pursue goals, we restore confidence and control to our lives. For example:

» Shon restored control when he trained himself on the law and built mentor relationships,

» Michael restored control when he worked to earn academic credentials, begin a publishing career, and open businesses,

» I restored control when I began working with Michael to create content that would launch my consulting career.

With more control, people have less dependence on the system. By controlling our decisions, the less we depend on the system or others. We leave the pains of confinement behind. We're taking action and restoring confidence.

By creating mental escapes with personal activities that are productive, people minimize prison frustrations. Reading and writing can help. These activities bring connection and lead to learning, which may lessen the pain of confinement by building a sense of productivity and industriousness. Time passes slowly when people feel as if they're wasting it.

Time-management skills help people grow through confinement. Serve the sentence with an eye toward the future, actually visualizing achievements during a given time frame. Think in terms of weeks, months, years, and decades. What can you do today to ensure your life is stronger, better in time periods ahead?

Every day may feel like a challenge. Yet by pursuing specific goals, people empower themselves. Our course on The Straight-A Guide can help. Learn more about our Straight-A Guide Course at ReslientCourses.com. A values-based, goal-oriented adjustment helps people stay away from the ocean of problems that so easily drown people in prison.

Another strategy may include keeping a journal to identify goals in specific time frames. From those goals, people can reverse engineer progress points, or milestones. People that know where they want to be in ten years should know what they should achieve in five years.

They also should have three-year plans, with a complete understanding of how both the three and five-year milestones relate to the ten-year vision. When a person knows where he wants to be in three, five, and ten years, then it is easier for him to understand where he needs to be in one year. And if he can see the one-year goal, where does the individual need to be in six months? In three months?

Our team members always used long-term goals as beacons of light. They helped us through the journey, and we're still using this strategy now.

We encourage you to do the same.

Final Word:

Prison, like anywhere else in life is about making choices and understanding ramifications accompany choices we make. Some people choose to build an image inside fences that result in their leaving prison far less able to succeed upon release than when they began their term. A smaller percentage of people grow during confinement and move on to enjoy fulfilling lives.

People in prison should not expect to find any reward for their efforts to improve, to grow, or to redeem themselves. The system makes few provisions to incentivize personal growth, although we're hopeful with the First Step Act.

Expect punitive conditions in prison. Despite those conditions, identify specific goals to achieve, then figure out how to reach them—regardless of obstacles that will surface.

Be prepared!